DON'T YOU KNOW? HAVEN'T YOU HEARD?

The Life Story of Eric B. Hare

R. Curtis Barger

mrs. Malenda

REVIEW AND HERALD PUBLISHING ASSOCIATION
Washington, DC 20039-0555
Hagerstown, MD 21740

Copyright © 1985 by Review and Herald Publishing
Association
Editor: Raymond H. Woolsey
Book design: Richard Steadham
Cover art: Jeff Dever

Printed in U.S.A.

Library of Congress Cataloging in Publication Data

Barger, R. Curtis.
    Don't you know? haven't you heard?

    1. Hare, Eric B. 2. Missionaries—Burma—Biography.
3. Missionaries—Australia—Biography. 4. Seventh-day
Adventists—United States—Clergy—Biography.
I. Title.
BV3271.H33B37 1985 266'.6732'0924 [B] 85-11920

ISBN 0-8280-0278-9

CONTENTS

Eric B. Hare

Foreword

This is not *my* story, and I promise to stay out of the way so it will come through as the unique story of Eric B. Hare, a truly remarkable man. However, in a sense, for those who knew "Dr. Rabbit" personally, his story is their story too, for his was an unusually strong influence.

His influence on me began several decades ago when I was a church pastor in the Hawaiian Islands and Elder Hare came to assist in junior camps, and later to conduct a child evangelism institute. Some time after that, as a Sabbath school department director in Central California, I gained new insights and great inspiration as I assisted him in Sabbath school workshops.

At the 1962 session of the General Conference of Seventh-day Adventists, held in San Francisco, I was asked to join the General Conference Sabbath School Department in Washington, D.C., as an associate director to succeed Elder Hare. So here I found myself seated in the very same old uncomfortable swivel chair, behind the very same desk, in the very same small office that he had occupied for many years. And I was both amused and humbled many times in the early months of my tenure there.

Guides from the Public Relations Department would escort visitors on tours of the General Conference complex. I would hear them coming down the hall toward my room, and as they drew near I would hear the guide say, "And this next room is where Eric B. Hare used to be." Some of the more bold visitors— or perhaps the more curious to see just what kind of creature would be presumptuous enough to sit where Eric B. Hare had sat—would pop in long enough to say, "Oh, so *you* have taken Elder Hare's place." And I would hasten to protest, "Oh, no! I have only *succeeded* him; no one can ever take *his* place! I don't have his big black bushy eyebrows and I don't have what is back of his eyebrows!"

In a capsule, this is why the story of Eric B. Hare is especially significant. He was unique as a person, not only because he was blessed with great natural gifts, talents, and abilities but because he was so willing and so dedicated in using and improving what God had given him for the benefit and blessing of others. His story is being told, not in adulation of the man, but to encourage imitation. I believe that in all modesty he could have said, as did the apostle Paul, "Wherefore I beseech you, be ye followers of me." "Be ye followers of me, even as I also am of Christ" (1 Cor. 4:16; 11:1).

Elder Hare was intelligent, practical in skills, adaptable, and humble. He had the unique ability of truly great persons to look at life from a child's viewpoint. Perhaps he will be remembered most for two outstanding qualities—seemingly unbounded enthusiasm and an active, vivid imagination. He had a graphic pictorial style of writing and speaking. He knew how to clothe bare narrative, the lifeless body of actual facts, with garments of real-life thought, speaking, and action. The result was never dull, and often very exciting.

In His public ministry Jesus used parables extensively, telling short stories about familiar objects and happenings with apt application to real life. In this dedicated use of one of God's gifts, as well as in his use of other talents and abilities, Elder Hare followed his divine-human Model, the Master Storyteller, Teacher, and Healer.

The title of this book derives from an oft-repeated double or triple question that became a hallmark of Eric Hare, storyteller par excellence. "Don't you know? Haven't you heard? Hasn't anyone told you?" And when these tantalizing questions were asked in person, accompanied by the high arching of his thick black eyebrows, it was virtually impossible to avoid a breathless anticipation of what would be coming next. When we think of these questions in the context of the good-news story of the gospel, we see how pertinent and effective they can be as attention-arousing openers. Certainly it was in this context that Elder Hare became such an appealing bearer of the gospel's good tidings.

Introduction

"The old jungle village headman leaned forward, lowered his voice to a whisper, raised a warning finger, and said, 'Haven't you heard? Don't you know? Hasn't anyone ever told you? The place is cursed. The treasure is cursed. The one who tries to take it shall perish in the attempt.'

"The headman told the story of the jealous villagers and the two years of famine, the story of the cursed pagoda and the buried treasure, and the death of the two daring hunters. Then he added, 'You had better not build a mission station there. You could not live there, in the first place; and you could never get anyone from this part of the world to go to a school or a hospital that you might build at Ohn Daw.'

"'Ha, ha, ha! Mr. Headman, we are not afraid of the curses or evil spirits. We worship a God who is stronger than all the forces of evil, and we feel that God wants us to build a mission station in that place. Will you please give us the address of the nearest government official where we can obtain permission to use the old village site for a mission station?'

"In three weeks we had the letter granting permission to build at the old village site of Ohn Daw, 'The Cluster of Palm Trees.' We began clearing our border lines through the jungle. As we cut, suddenly there loomed up before us a jungle-covered mound. "'Elder

Hamilton, what's this?' I said.

"We moved closer with our brush hooks, tore away some of the tangled creepers, and found broken bricks. Our eyes bulged a little. 'It is the old haunted pagoda, Brother Hamilton,' I said. 'Are you scared?'

" 'No, come on, let's climb up on it,' he replied. Up over the rocks of the foundation we climbed, cutting and clearing the tall grass and the creepers and the little trees as we went. There before our eyes we beheld a great tree growing out of the very top of it. It was the post that the young men had embedded in the heart of the pagoda years and years before. Now it had grown roots and branches, and waved its long arms from the top of the broken ruins. Right into the foundation was the hole where two hunters had lost their lives digging for the buried treasure.

"Down into the hole we jumped. We felt a long way from everywhere. I looked at Brother Hamilton, and he looked at me. 'Let's dig for the treasure,' I said. But before we could start we heard a low grumbling, growling sound that increased in volume for a second or two till it ended with a dull thud at our very feet! My hair stood on end! My eyes bulged!"

Eric B. Hare has just concluded the evening campfire story at Wawona Youth Camp. More than a hundred pairs of eyes are fastened on him as the suspense mounts and reaches its climax amid a chorus of groans, "We have to wait till tomorrow night to hear what happened." Of course, tomorrow night they will find out what happened at the haunted pagoda, but the suspense will mount to another climax to be continued at the campfire program the following night.

Who was this jungle storyteller and author who thrilled audiences, young and old alike, for more than sixty years? This book is his story!

His
1 "Hare-itage"

Eric B. Hare was born on October 12, 1894, in Hawthorn, a suburb of Melbourne, Australia. He was the second of five children born to Robert and Henrietta Hare. How he happened to be born in far-off Australia with an American mother and an Irish father requires an explanation.

Eric's father, Robert, was born in northern Ireland, but in 1863, along with his father, Joseph; his mother, Maggie; and his nine brothers and sisters, he emigrated to New Zealand. Robert was just 5 years old when the family arrived in Auckland to start life in their new world.

Within a few years a baby sister was added to the family, and shortly afterward Mother Maggie Hare fell ill and died. Little Robert seemed especially devastated by the loss of his mother. For two days he wept or moved silently as if lost and in a daze. Then he brought to his father a little poem he had written about his mother and her loving care. It was his first poem, but it was not his last, for in his long lifetime he wrote hundreds of poems, expressing in this way his innermost emotions and aspirations.

Joseph Hare, with eleven motherless children, later married Hannah Skinner, a physician and close friend of the Hare family. She had eight fatherless children. Now instead of eleven children there were nineteen! Quite a houseful! But there were more to come. Five more, so that Father Joseph Hare became known all around the area as the Irishman with twenty-four children!

In 1885 pioneer Seventh-day Adventist missionary S. N. Haskell visited New Zealand, preaching the good news of the gospel and selling such books as *The Great Controversy* and *Daniel and the Revelation*. Robert Hare was one of the early converts. He decided then to give up his shipbuilding business and become a preacher. Haskell recommended that he go to Healdsburg College in California to prepare for the ministry.

Meanwhile, during the time that Robert was growing up in New Zealand, his future bride and lifelong companion was growing up in far-off America. Her father, George Taylor Johnson, inherited a large cotton-and-tobacco plantation near New Orleans and fought in the Confederate army until he was severely wounded. After his medical discharge he returned to the plantation, only to find the home burned to the ground. He sold out and went to New York City to seek his fortune, finally becoming captain of a steamship on the Hudson River. He married Sophie Lansletter, a fine young woman whose parents had migrated from Baden, Germany. To this couple a daughter was born, whom they named Henrietta.

As Henrietta grew up she loved to attend and participate in Sunday school and the church service in the local Church of England. She was a bright student with a questioning mind. At the age of 11 she heard the minister read the fourth commandment, and it suddenly dawned on her that the seventh day of the week is the Sabbath. "Why, the seventh day is Saturday," she said to herself. "We must be keeping the wrong day!"

The Johnson family moved to California, where Henrietta took a year of teacher training. At the age of

18 she was hired to teach a small public school at Dow's Prairie, about fourteen miles north of Eureka, California. An evangelist by the name of McClure asked permission to hold some Sunday meetings in the schoolhouse, which was readily granted.

Henrietta determined to attend the Sunday meetings to make sure he didn't teach things that were not in harmony with her Bible. She was pleased and impressed at how plain and logical were the messages the preacher presented. This encouraged her to ask him the questions about the Sabbath that had puzzled her for years. The evangelist hesitated, fearing to prejudice her before she had a better background, but the young teacher pressed him for answers, declaring that no one, including her pastor, had given her answers that agreed with the Bible.

Pastor McClure responded, "If you are going to follow the Bible, Miss Johnson, then Saturday is the day you should keep."

Henrietta was startled for a moment, then looked the preacher straight in the eye and asked, "Well, you're a minister. Why don't *you* keep Saturday for the Sabbath?" When evangelist McClure replied, "I do," the young woman was shocked and excited.

Pastor McClure showed her the books *The Great Controversy* and *Matthew Twenty-four*, and she bought and read them eagerly. She began almost at once to keep the Sabbath, but her parents did not share her enthusiasm. Instead, they accused her of being out of her mind. They were relieved when she visited friends in a neighboring town for a week, and hoped the friends would set her straight. But her friends invited her to go with them to some meetings held by a minister named Loughborough, and how surprised and delighted she was to meet Pastor McClure at those meetings!

Although Henrietta had been religious, she now

realized that some of the pleasures and fashions of the world were a strong influence in her life. She determined, by God's grace, to renounce these personal idols, and she made a full commitment to the Lord. On December 10, 1884, she was baptized.

Elder McClure said, "Miss Johnson, the Lord needs young women of your talent and ability. Why don't you go down to our Healdsburg College and take the Bible instructor's course? It's not very far away. I believe that the Lord will help you win many people to Christ."

On the very day Henrietta decided to attend Healdsburg College, Robert Hare, all unbeknownst to her, of course, set sail for America. Henrietta enrolled in the Bible instructor's course but was soon pressed into service to teach mathematics in the place of a teacher who could not come. This made her a member of the faculty.

In this faculty role, Henrietta met and chatted with Robert Hare, just arrived from New Zealand. Students had heard he was coming, and there had been much conjecture about what kind of person Robert would be. Some speculated that he might be a Maori or someone of a different race. Little by little, in casual conversations as they sat at the same table in the dining room, Robert and Henrietta learned of each other's background and experience. Their common meeting ground was their recent conversion to the Seventh-day Adventist way of life.

On the morning of May 22, 1888, Robert was ordained to the gospel ministry. That afternoon the marriage ceremony for Robert and Henrietta was conducted by Elder McClure, and the next day Elder and Mrs. Robert Hare set sail from San Francisco on their honeymoon voyage to New Zealand. Henrietta never returned to the United States, but she never forgot that she was an American. Her children remember that every Fourth of July she would put her little American flag on the table and invite other Americans over to celebrate the American holiday.

The honeymoon may have officially ended on June 15, 1888, when Robert and Henrietta arrived in Auckland, but for this couple, so much in love with each other and with their Lord, it was the beginning of a deeper lifetime romance of gospel ministry together. They joined Elder and Mrs. A. G. Daniells in Auckland for a series of meetings. A year later their cup of joy was full when a son, Reuben, was born to them.

So the months passed as Robert filled the difficult role of evangelist, revivalist, personal worker, and writer. His days were more than full, but by his side through it all was Henrietta. Even when he must be away for special meetings, it was she who carried on the visiting and the giving of Bible studies. From the time he was 2 weeks old, baby Reuben was taken along to the meetings, where his mother played the organ or performed other duties.

The Hares were called from place to place to conduct evangelistic meetings, and Robert became a powerful preacher. In 1894 they were in the Melbourne area in Australia. It was here that Eric Burnham Hare was born.

2 "As the Twig Is Bent"

"And when I grow up—" *"And when I grow up—"* "may I be a missionary—" *"may I be a missionary—"* "at one of the four corners of the earth—" *"at one of the four corners of the earth—"* "preaching the gospel—" *"preaching the gospel."* As far back as Eric could remember, he had repeated this prayer, phrase by phrase, at his mother's knee as she taught him to pray. When he began to form his own prayers, and later as a college student, this special prayer was the focus of his private devotions.

Father Robert would play a game with Eric and his little sister, Ruth. "Shall we play church again this evening?" Eric would dance for joy. "I'll be the horse," his father would say, "and you can be the preacher. I'll carry you to your church." On his hands and knees, with Eric on his back, Father would gallop around the room until they came to a big chair. "Here's your church," he would say. While the boy situated himself on the chair, Father would gather little sister Ruth, two or three dolls, and the kitten. The horse then became part of the congregation, and Eric would sing and sing and preach and preach. When the service ended, Father would change back into the horse to take the young preacher back home, and then, Eric was off to bed.

These direct, immediate influences "bent the twig," giving a special inclination to the tree of Eric's developing life. The sturdy but gentle Christian qualities of his Irish father, and the courageous but refining nature of his American mother, greatly helped the growing boy to determine his life's ideals and goals.

In addition to cultivating an ambition to become a preacher and a missionary, Eric's parents encouraged a love for music. They provided instruments and instruction so that each of their children learned to play at a very early age. Another of Eric's early memories was of his father and older brother, Reuben, joining the Bible Echo Publishing Company's brass band, Father with a big E-flat bass horn and Reuben with a baritone. It is easy to picture the distraught mother trying to endure the loud, monotonous sounds of father and son practicing long each day on their big horns. But when she saw Eric trying to make sounds on the bass horn, it was not long before she had taught him to play hymns on a cornet. Before he was 5 years old the family had their own brass band. As we shall see later, music was to play a significant part in Eric's carrying out his lifelong dreams. He was ever grateful that his mother had been encouraging and persistent in giving him cornet lessons each day over a period of many months.

The Robert Hare family were excited one day to receive a letter from Susie Fulton. Robert and Henrietta first knew John Fulton and Susie Newlon when they were fellow students at Healdsburg College, and since that time they had become the closest of friends. Now the Fultons were missionaries in Fiji. Susie's letter enclosed a family picture. There were the father, John; the mother, Susie; Jessie, 7 years old; Agnes, 5½ years old; and Georgie, 2 years old.

Robert gazed fondly at the picture. "Fancy Susie and John having two girls and one boy."

"Yes, and we have two boys and one girl! Robin [her

pet name for her husband], wouldn't it be interesting if—"

"If what?"

"Oh—nothing!"

After this, Eric looked at the picture frequently, until Jessie and Agnes and Georgie seemed to be a part of the family, especially when his mother told stories of school days at Healdsburg.

When on August 16, 1896, little Ruth came to join the Robert Hare family, there had been great joy. Now, as the months of May and June, 1899, went by, although Eric was not really aware of what was going on, his mother used every spare moment making little dresses and knitting booties. Much to the disappointment of all, they learned that Robert must be away at a special conference all the last half of July, the very time when another "blessed event" was scheduled to take place. But Reuben had become a young man, 10 years old. He was taken into the family's confidence and pressed into service to run the two miles to Nurse Green's house in the middle of the night to say she was needed immediately at the Hare house.

All went well. By 6:00 A.M. on that July day in 1899, another little sister came to join the happy family. Mother named her Roberta, after her husband, Robert. Father wanted to name the baby Henrietta, after her mother. In the end she became known as Nettie.

At the age of 6, Eric joined the Echo Publishing Company's brass band, standing on a box to play the cornet part. The band was conducted by a professional bandmaster and was one of several brass bands in the city that performed at various civic functions. When the Duke of York—later to become the Prince of Wales and then King George V of England—visited Australia, the Echo Brass Band was given a place to perform on the procession route. The band members practiced long and arduously and were in position by 9:00 A.M. The procession was to start at ten o'clock, but it was actually after four in the afternoon when the duke and accompanying dignitaries came by and the Echo Band performed. But the duke, riding in the royal carriage, looked right at the band, tipped his hat, and smiled. Eric declared that although they had waited so long and had missed their noonday meal, they weren't tired anymore and they weren't hungry anymore. They had seen the Duke of York!

Involvement in such activities at an early age, and being given responsibility for specific parts, did much to train Eric for a life of efficient, dedicated service. One day his father said, "Eric, I want you to come with me to the city. I want you to help me choose a cornet for little Ruth to play." This note of confidence created within Eric a healthy and satisfying feeling of self-worth. Five-year-old Ruth did very well in learning to play the instrument, and it was not long until the Hare family had a five-piece brass band.

In July, 1902, the Robert Hare family entered an exciting period of evangelism. Revival meetings were held in some established churches, but preaching in the tent was mainly to nonmembers. Crusades were held in ten or more cities. Previously, when Evangelist Hare had held meetings in the "calico church" he had only Henrietta at the organ to assist him. Now he had a brass band whose members had practiced until they performed like professionals. The band was a chief attraction. Reuben, 13, played bass on his baritone; Eric, 8, played soprano on his cornet; Ruth, 6½, played alto on her cornet. Mother Hare played the organ, and Evangelist Hare was bandmaster and played the tenor part on his clarinet, having given up the tuba because it was too big to carry from place to place.

Eric probably contributed his share of live-wire boyish pranks, but by the time he turned 10 years old he had done more than play his cornet at his father's meetings. He began to be interested greatly in the preaching, taking notes and making sketches of his father's visual object lessons and teaching aids. His father used many illustrations, based on simple familiar things, to make truth clear and easy to apply. These ideas and skills Eric would use later in a masterful way in his ministry. It was at the Stawell series that Eric found his heart stirred with a new love for Jesus and was baptized into the church.

Every growing boy or girl adopts a hero or heroine, a role model who becomes very meaningful in setting life's aspirations and goals. Eric was fortunate to have chosen at an early age to look at life pretty much through the eyes of his sturdy and gifted father and his loving and godly mother. Their pioneer spirit and their utmost devotion to a career of serving and saving others certainly affected the choices Eric made as he matured.

John and Susie Fulton also helped set the mold upon Eric's lifework. The Hares and the Fultons had kept in close touch ever since college days together. John and Susie became dedicated and effective missionaries in Fiji, and they took every opportunity to share their enthusiasm for mission service.

About the time of Eric's baptism a letter from Susie in Fiji bore the sad news of the death of their little Georgie, just 7 years old. Eric's father and mother shed sympathetic tears and recounted how, in spite of sickness and sadness, the Fultons had proved to be genuine missionaries. Eric thrilled at the thought that he might serve in a similar way.

Another incident helped in a profound way to establish Eric's faith in the way God loves and leads His people. His father was still engaged in the Stawell series when he became ill. There were signs of deep depression, accompanied by a digestive upset and progressive weakness. Finally one day he declared that he had no strength to preach that evening. Mother Henrietta sought to comfort and encourage him, reminding him that Jesus taught His followers to pray for daily bread, and that surely we may ask Him to provide daily strength to carry on. She and the children would pray for him; she believed that God would hear and reward their faith so he would be able to preach.

Mother Henrietta tells what happened: "One morning a letter came from America. It was written in green ink. When we opened it we found it was from Sister E. G. White. She wrote at half past two in the morning when everyone in the house was asleep. The Lord awakened her and told her she must write to Robert Hare in Australia at once and put the letter in the morning mail. She was directed to encourage him to hold on to his work, for his work is not done yet, and as long as he keeps humble the Lord will use him. Sister White was shown the tent crowded with people, with angels moving up and down among the people and an angel standing beside him."

Surely, here was a miracle in answer to prayer. Soon the illness and weakness were gone, and Father carried on his meetings, full of faith and courage. Ever afterward Eric carried with him the mental picture of angels moving among the listeners, and a mighty angel standing beside the speaker when the gospel message was proclaimed.

When on July 17, 1905, Enid Lucy was born to the Hare family, the older children began at once to speculate as to what instrument the new arrival would play in the family band. In any case, the family brass band continued to provide a musical attraction to their father's meetings as they moved from place to place. When they moved to Adelaide in South Australia, in September, 1906, the Hare family was pleased to have Alma Butz, daughter of the local conference president, join their brass band, playing the euphonium. At the age of 12, Alma was already a talented and versatile musician. In time she married Norman Wiles, and together they became missionaries to the New Hebrides.

Let us go back a bit in history as it has to do with the Hare family. In 1894 a site was chosen for the Avondale School. At first an old hotel building was rented, with workers and male students living in tents. Just two classes were offered in 1895. Metcalfe Hare, Eric's uncle, was asked to be the business manager and treasurer. Persons familiar in denominational history were part of the scene in the early development of Avondale, such as Herbert Lacey, S. N. Haskell, and C. B. Hughes.

When Ellen G. White moved onto the school property and built her home, known as Sunnyside, workers were much encouraged by her counsel and guidance. On October 5, 1896, she laid the cornerstone for the girls' dormitory, the first building to be erected on the Avondale campus. The first year after the formal opening of the school, April 28, 1897, sixty students enrolled, at a time when there were only about 750 Seventh-day Adventists in all of Australia. These early believers exhibited extraordinary faith and courage.

For four years Avondale received the personal prophetic guidance and encouragement of Mrs. E. G. White. Eric always recalled with great satisfaction that Avondale provided balanced education of head, heart, and hand—a training for practical, effective service in God's cause. In 1900 Sister White returned to the United States.

It was always gratifying to Eric to realize how much

his uncle Metcalfe contributed to the developing work of the church. Metcalfe Hare served as business manager and treasurer at Avondale for twelve years. During that time he built a motor launch to connect the school with the railway station on Dora Creek, about three miles away. He also supervised the building of a health-food factory, converted from an old sawmill. This enterprise provided wholesome food for the early Adventists and much-needed labor for Avondale students.

As the number of churches and members in Australia grew, so did the number of sudents at Avondale. It soon became apparent that Pastor L. A. Hoopes, the Bible instructor, must be relieved of some of his load, for he was also the pastor of the large village church. Thus the union committee voted to ask Pastor Robert Hare to be the Bible teacher at Avondale School.

It was exciting news for Eric and his family. They all looked forward eagerly to the move. "Reuben can live with us, and we'll have our whole family together again," said Mother.

"And I'll have Reuben to help me make a rowboat so we can have picnics on the creek," said Father.

"Goody, goody," shouted Eric and his three sisters.

"And Eric can play in the school band," said his father.

Eric could scarcely contain his excitement and delight.

Then came the day when, with a few pieces of packing-case furniture and personal effects, the Robert Hare family boarded the train, bound for the Dora Creek station and Avondale School. They had looked at their old tables, chairs, and beds and had decided to have an auction, thinking the value of the furniture would not be worth the cost of moving it. The auctioneer did his best, but the family netted only twelve pounds (about $60 at that time)—hardly a magnificent sum.

To reach Dora Creek they had to change trains twice—from narrow gauge to modern broad gauge and then to standard gauge. Students from the school met them and helped load their things onto the motor launch. Father Robert quickly observed that the launch had been built by his brother Metcalfe. In about an hour they were unloaded at the school wharf.

The next morning as the family stood in line in the school dining room, Eric was somewhat bewildered by all the bustle, laughter, and conversation. Suddenly he saw his mother turn quickly and exclaim, "Oh, look, there's Susie's girl!" She grabbed and hugged a lovely young woman. "Oh, Agnes, I'd know you anywhere! You're just like your mother when I first knew her! Is Jessie here?"

"Yes," answered Agnes, "she's coming." In a few minutes another girl came, looking just like Agnes, except she was about one size larger.

At the sound of a bell all were silent as someone returned thanks for the food. Eric's mother chatted a few more moments with the girls—and that is about all Eric could remember later about that occasion. He had met Susie's girls and he knew that the younger one was about his age, but for some time to come Agnes was just "Susie's girl."

There followed busy, joyous, thrilling days as the Hare family moved into a village house near the church. Reuben came home from his summer work, school began its next session, Father started his new teaching assignment, and Eric was invited to play first cornet in the school band and orchestra. He could scarcely comprehend how he, a boy of 13, would be asked to play first cornet!

His father had an answer to that: "My boy, the Good Book says, 'A man's gift maketh room for him, and bringeth him before great men,' and it's true. During the past six years you have been doing more than just helping me with the music. You have been developing your talent. Now you are beginning to reap your reward." Those words encouraged Eric, and he realized he was growing up.

When Charles Watson and his family moved into the house next door to the Hares, Eric began a rather unusual and meaningful experience. Mr. Watson, a successful businessman, had recently heard and accepted the message taught by Seventh-day Adventists. After his baptism, he felt he was being called to the ministry. So here Mr. Watson was, taking the ministerial course and in Bible classes with Eric even though he was a mature man with four children. He and 15-year-old Eric became chums as they walked to and from school together. Charles Watson greatly admired Eric's father, so much so that he not only learned Bible truths the instructor taught but began to imitate Pastor Hare's mannerisms and style of delivery. We can well imagine how pleased Eric and his father were years later to learn that Charles Watson had been asked to serve the church as its General Conference president (1930-1936).

Eric was to look back to 1909 as being a very special year. Elder Fulton, missionary to Fiji, was asked to be president of the Australasian Union Conference. Jessie and Agnes Fulton were living in the school dormitory. One day the two Fulton girls came to visit Eric's mother. Eric felt uncomfortable in the presence of girls, so he kept out of sight. Then his mother called, "Eric, I need some nice ripe figs for supper. Here, take Agnes and show her the orchard, and pick her some nice figs while you are getting some for me. She handed Agnes a saucepan, and Eric showed the girl the fruit trees and vines, then began to pick figs.

Agnes showed no interest in the orchard. She was more interested in teasing Eric about one of the girls at school. He was long to remember the short conversation that ensued.

"But you do like her, don't you?" she insisted.

"Here's another lovely fig for you," he answered. "Don't you like figs?"

"Yes, but I told her I was going to ask you. Now tell me, Eric, you do like her, don't you?"

He looked down at Agnes from his perch in the fig tree. They had been in classes together for two years. Now suddenly it was as if he had never before seen this gorgeous creature.

"You do like her, don't you?" Agnes persisted.

Eric's heart thumped, he felt a warm glow on his cheeks, and his mouth was dry. Finally words came. "No, Agnes, I like you!"

At that, the girl jumped up and ran away. To Eric she was never again "Susie's girl." She was *his* girl.

For a time Eric was able to see Agnes quite often, at least briefly, as he went by the Fulton cottage on his way to and from work with other boys to cut wood to fire the health-food factory boiler. But when Elder and Mrs. Fulton moved nearer the center of his work as union president and the girls moved into the dormitory, contacts with Agnes were much less frequent.

This disappointed Eric, but for the Hare family the year 1911 turned out to be a happy and profitable one. Near the end of the school year Eric overheard his father tell his mother that this would be the end of his fourth year at the school and that he expected to be called back into public evangelism. His mother seemed to feel the same way about it. Although it would mean another move, she would continue to be happy.

Suddenly a sober thought struck Eric's parents. It was unlikely that the family would ever be together again as an entire family. Reuben would graduate and be married at the close of the school year. The parents would be on the move again in evangelism. Eric would remain in Avondale for two more years. Wisely, Father suggested that they should have a picture taken of the entire family. They did, and the photograph of that entire beautiful family has been a precious treasure ever since.

His
3 "Special Place"

Eric's mother sought to focus his aspirations and plans on finding God's will in the matter of mission service, rather than simply to fulfill human ambition. She would say, "And remember, Eric, my son, Sister White says, 'Not more surely is the place prepared for us in the heavenly mansions than is the special place designated on earth where we are to work for God [*Christ's Object Lessons*, p. 327].' So, somewhere God has a *special* place for you where *you* can serve better than anyone else."

And Eric would whisper, "Where, Mother, where?"

"Oh, somewhere," his mother would reply, "and when you find that place, you will know."

When in 1913 Eric graduated from Avondale College, he was still praying to be a missionary and was seeking to discover where his "special place" might be. One thing he knew for sure—he was in love with Agnes Fulton and expected to marry her someday. And he was quite sure that since her parents, John and Susie Fulton, had been such great pioneer missionaries in Fiji, Fiji would naturally be his "special place."

When Eric's name came up for placement in the work, the union committee counseled him to take the two-year male nurse's course being offered at the Sydney Sanitarium. Knowing of his desire for mission service, they felt the course was advisable not just for the sake of the work but also for Eric's sake, because he might be stationed far from a doctor or a hospital. Eric was glad to enroll.

By March, 1915, with just six more months to go on the course, Eric was also making good progress learning the Fijian language, coached by his bride-to-be, Agnes. About this time Elder A. G. Daniells came to Australia to study ways to reorganize the work of the church. Elder Fulton introduced Eric to the visiting church dignitary, saying, "This young man is going to be my son-in-law." This sounded good to Eric.

Elder Daniells shook his hand. "I'm glad to know you, Eric," he said, and Eric felt as if the man's eyes were looking straight through him. "Are you Pastor Robert Hare's son?"

"Yes."

About through the nurse's course, are you?"

"Yes."

That was a very brief exchange between an inexperienced youth and the president of the General Conference, but Eric dared hope Elder Daniells might help him fulfill his lifelong dream to be a missionary.

Elder Daniells did help, sooner than anyone might have expected and in a way Eric did not anticipate. From Australia, Elder Daniells had gone to visit India. A few weeks went by; then a cablegram came from Elder Daniells to Elder Fulton. It read:

"WE NEED A YOUNG MEDICAL MISSIONARY FOR A NEW MISSION STATION AMONG THE KAREN SPIRIT WORSHIPERS OF BURMA. WILL ERIC AND AGNES ACCEPT THE INVITATION?"

Both Eric and Agnes gasped in astonishment when the message was read to them.

"Burma?"

"What about Fiji?"

"Where is Burma?"

For Agnes the long-held dream of mission service in Fiji with Eric did not fade quickly. "Maybe we'd better take time to pray about this to be sure Burma is where God wants us," she proposed.

All was silent as each searched his heart, trying to think through what it would mean to answer the question of the cabled message. Then Eric slowly gave voice to his inner feelings: "I don't need to pray anymore about it. You know I've been praying ever since I can remember for the Lord to let me be a missionary somewhere out in the four corners of the earth. I believe that God makes known His will through the leaders of His church. The way Elder Daniells looked at me when he was here, I just knew something was about to happen, and now I'm ready to go to Burma if that is where the Lord wants me. What do you think, Agnes?"

There were tears in her eyes, but they were brave tears. "'Whither thou goest, I will go,'" Agnes answered softly.

On June 24, 1915, Eric Hare and Agnes Fulton were married. Eric's course in nursing was finished in September, and in October of that year the newlyweds sailed off to Burma, land of golden pagodas and Karen spirit worshipers. As family and friends said Goodbye to the young medical missionaries there were sad tears and there were glad tears. With a choked voice and trembling lips Eric's mother said to him, "I may never see you again on this earth, my son, but this is another of the happiest days of my life. God has heard my prayers. My son is going to the ends of the earth to preach the gospel!"

Her sentiments were echoed by Eric's father. "God has been good to us. We have one son in the tent work. He has already held five evangelistic campaigns and built up three churches. And now my second son is going out as a missionary to the ends of the earth. God is good! God is good!"

By train and ship Eric and Agnes made their way to Burma, with brief stops in Colombo, Madras, and Calcutta. They arrived in Rangoon, Burma, on October 31, 1915. They were greeted at the wharf by Pastor George Hamilton, superintendent of the Karen Mission, and by Mary Gibbs, the missionary dispensary nurse. Soon the new missionaries were being regaled by fascinating and sometimes exciting stories of how God opened the way to secure land upon which the new Karen Mission might be established. Located at Kamamaung, on the banks of the Salween River, the mission at that point consisted only of temporary houses where the Hamiltons and Miss Gibbs lived. Permanent houses and the dispensary were being built, and medical aid was already being given by the nurse, in the shade of big mango trees.

It was obvious that Nurse Gibbs had more than she could handle in caring for the sick and suffering people who came each day. Eric wished heartily that she could stay. She had had much practical experience and could speak in the Karen language. But it was for these reasons that she had been asked to develop a new school for girls as soon as possible. And it was for these reasons that Eric and Agnes had been called to be medical assistants at this new station.

"First, you will be given six months for language study here in Rangoon," Pastor Hamilton explained. "Then it will be time to roll up your sleeves and get right into your work at the station. By that time the dispensary and your bamboo house will be built."

Alone that first evening in Burma, Eric raised his luxuriant black eyebrows to look quizzically at his bride. She looked at him with eyes revealing the questions in her own mind. What would the future hold for them? Was this truly the "special place" that would answer Eric's lifelong prayers?

Six months went by quickly. The Hares could speak Karen enough to get by in most situations and could read the Karen Bible, at least haltingly. They traveled by river steamer and motor launch to the mission station. A little bamboo and leaf house was ready, and they quickly settled into it with their few belongings.

Eric rolled up his sleeves and reported to Nurse Gibbs at the dispensary. Her warm smile of welcome put him somewhat at ease. She pointed to a doctor's white jacket hanging behind the door. When he turned to look at the patients lined up on the veranda, he was dismayed. Perhaps twenty persons waited their turn; some proudly displayed their bandages as they described what the white woman "doctor" had done for them.

There was an unsettling array of tropical ailments from which men, women, and children were suffering: sore eyes, ringworm, fever, ugly ulcers, and in children, evidence of stomach disorders such as worms.

Nurse Gibbs spoke pleasantly. "Here's a man who needs to have a tooth pulled, Doctor. How about you doing it for him?"

Self-confidence melted quickly. Pull a tooth? Doctor? He knew very well that he was not a medical doctor. His training had been only as a nurse. Of course, he had found that the Karen word for *doctor* was used for all professional people. He certainly felt no elation at being called a doctor, but rather a deep sense of inadequacy, inasmuch as the nurse's course had not included dentistry. "But, Miss Gibbs," he whispered, "I've never pulled a tooth in all my—"

Miss Gibbs exhibited no sympathy at all. "Here are the forceps, the oil of cloves, and the lance and elevator if you need them." She placed the small tray of instruments in his hands. "And there is your patient!"

Describing this abrupt initiation into medical missionary work for the jungle folk, Elder Hare wrote:

"There was no way out. After all, was not this what I had come to Burma to do? All right, then, I would do it. I asked the patient to open his mouth and show me the tooth. Fortunately, it was a first molar, easy to get at, and it was very loose. I picked up a small swab and dipped it in the oil of cloves. I noticed that my hand was trembling. That would never do. Me, a strong young man, trembling! I painted around the tooth with the oil of cloves and said to myself, 'Mr. Hare, control yourself! Control yourself!' But it did no good. The trembling extended to my arms. I picked up the forceps, and by the time I had fastened them on the tooth, my knees were knocking together. I broke out with cold perspiration all over, then suddenly the tooth was out! I'm not quite sure yet whether I pulled that tooth or whether it just fell out with the trembling."

Once that first tooth had been pulled and the grateful old man had gone, Nurse Gibbs turned to Eric with a smile and remarked, "Well, Doctor, you lived through that. Now see what that old man wants who has been sitting over there so patiently."

Someone, who evidently had been over the road, once said the three most essential qualifications a missionary should have are (1) adaptability, (2) adaptability, (3) adaptability. Eric began immediately to experience that maxim. If he and his bride were to help the Karen people, not only must they learn a new language, but they must also try to understand the Karens' superstitions and more primitive philosophy of life. As animists or spirit worshipers, the Karens explained everything that happened in terms of the influence or activity of the spirits that inhabited or manipulated various objects or forces of nature.

DYK-3

Eric sat beside the patient old man and asked, "What may I do for you?"

"I need some eye medicine," he said, pointing to one eye.

"Does it hurt?"

"No, not much, but I can't see out of it."

It was easy to see that the problem was a cataract, and Eric was about to tell the patient he must go to the government hospital in the city for that. But the old man continued to explain:

"Two years ago I had fever. My head was hot, but my feet were cold. Then one day the cold wind in my feet began to travel up my legs." He stood to show with motions how the cold wind went. "At last the cold wind came to the hot wind in my stomach. There was a terrible noise, and I thought I surely would die. But the cold wind kept on coming up and up, through my neck, over my head, and settled in my right eye. It has just gotten worse and worse, until now I can't see out of it at all."

Eric nodded soberly, although it was hard not to look amused.

"And so," the man continued, "I wish you could give me some wind medicine to drive that cold wind out of my eye down through my body, and out of my feet again. People tell me you have good wind medicine here." He was deadly serious.

The young missionary had to explain to the poor fellow that he would have to go to the government hospital in Moulmein, where they had the training and instruments that would take care of the cold wind in his eye. As the truth sank in, the old man turned slowly and went back into the jungle. It was a bitter disappointment, for he had no money and no way to travel so far.

It made Eric's heart ache, too. "I wish I were a real doctor," he said to Nurse Gibbs. "It was hard to tell him that we can't help. He was so disappointed."

"Yes," she agreed, "your heart will ache often, but you will find that we as nurses can take care of at least 90 percent of the ailments of these dear jungle people. Seeing how much they appreciate what we do will make your life here very rewarding.

Nurse Gibbs had had six years of experience in running a jungle dispensary; also, she had taken a special course in treating tropical diseases. During the next few weeks Eric learned a great deal that had not been included in his nurse's course. Miss Gibbs taught him to chart, diagnose, and treat diseases common to the jungle, such as malaria, dengue, and relapsing fever. She showed him how to lance boils, sew up wounds, and care for jungle accident cases, even amputating a limb to save a life. Eric soon discovered that his formal schooling had prepared him only to become educated in the practical school of experience. He was now thrust into the sea of tremendous human need, and for him it was sink or swim. He felt totally inadequate, but he learned quickly and trusted God to help him.

The work was far from exotic or glamorous. It might be a baby brought in who was crying with what the mother thought was a toothache, only to find that a tooth was almost rotted away, and when the fragments were removed, to discover three wriggling maggots in the infected area. Or it might be to answer a frantic call to a village three miles away to treat a man who had been "stung," only to find that the stung man had had one arm nearly torn off at the shoulder, the stinging having been done by an elephant. In the Karen language there is only one word for being stung by a bee or stuck by a pin or gored by an elephant's tusk.

Successfully caring for such unusual cases caused Eric to be happy and excited. He shared his exuberance with Miss Gibbs, and she smiled her approval and encouragement. "You'll make it, all right. Someday you will be a great jungle doctor."

One day as they chatted about their work, Miss Gibbs grinned broadly and asked, "Do you know what?"

"No, what?" Eric responded.

"The people keep asking what your name is," she said, "and I tell them it is Hare. But the word doesn't mean a thing to them. I try to explain its meaning in Karen, but their language makes no distinction between *hare* and *rabbit.* Then their eyes brighten up and their heads nod in approval, and they repeat, 'Thara Pa-Deh! Thara Pa-Deh!' That, you know, is 'Dr. Rabbit! Dr. Rabbit!' So don't be surprised to hear them calling you Dr. Rabbit someday."

Eric was delighted, and when he shared the news with Agnes, she too was greatly pleased. Both were puzzled, however, as to why the Karen liked that name especially. (In time, that too was made clear.) At least they felt they were being accepted and that they had indeed found their "special place" in God's great work.

In a rather gruesome episode that Eric called his jungle graduation exercise, the special significance of the title "Dr. Rabbit" was revealed. He was sleeping alone in his bamboo-and-leaf house. His wife and Nurse Gibbs were away for a day or two. It was about midnight. His day had been long and hard, so it took some time for him to awaken enough to realize that someone was calling, "Doctor! Doctor! Letter! Letter!"

Eric finally arose, looked out, and stood petrified at the sight of three almost naked men, bodies greased, holding gleaming knives in their right hands and small oil lamps in their left. It was a heart-stopping, eye-popping, hair-raising sight, and it took a few moments for the dazed young man to see that one of the men was holding a piece of paper and saying,

"Letter! Letter! Doctor! Doctor!"

In Eric's own words: "I swallowed hard, stroked my hair down, patted my ears back into position, then reached down and took the letter. Quickly I lighted my lamp and read:

"'Dear Mr. Hare:

"'An Indian marijuana addict has run amok here in Kamamaung, and has chopped up a Burmese woman and her 12-year-old son. Bring all your needles and sutures and see what you can do. BALDWIN

"'*Tenasserim District Forest Officer*'"

Eric knew Mr. Baldwin and other government men who often stayed at the rest house not far from the mission. Now thoroughly awake, he dressed quickly, loaded all the surgical supplies and medicines he had into his bag, and joined the greased-up messengers. He tried to get more information about the incident, but the Burmese men could not understand Karen, nor could he understand Burmese. They went single file through the jungle, two men in front of Eric and one behind. The Burmese men were all very tense; every crackling sound startled them. The long wicked-looking knives were held ready for instant action. Not only were they afraid of the crazed addict, but this was tiger country. Fortunately they met neither madman nor tiger, and in about twenty minutes arrived at the village.

The whole village was in a state of alarm; huge bonfires lighted the streets as if the villagers were trying to push back the terrifying darkness. The village headman met Eric and gave him the grisly details as they came to the house where the woman and her son were. "It's terrible," he said. "I don't know if they are still alive." He opened the door and pushed Eric inside, saying, "I can't bear to look at them," and closed the door.

In the dim light of his lantern Eric saw the mother

lying on a cotton mattress on the floor at one side of
the room, and the boy on another mattress on the
floor at the other side of the room. Eric had never seen
so much blood. The smell of it was strongly nauseat-
ing. All at once the boy began to yell, and the young
missionary knew that at least one of the victims was
alive. He stepped over the motionless body of the
mother. As he did so he stepped on the edge of her
mattress and he saw blood ooze out around his shoe.
His head began to swim, and he realized he was about
to faint. That would never do; he simply must not fall
in the middle of such a mess, so he talked out loud to
himself: "No, you don't, Dr. Rabbit. This is no time or
place to faint! Keep your wits about you!"

His lecture to himself worked. In a moment he was
comforting and caring for the frightened and severely
wounded boy, who had a deep gash in his neck.
Fortunately no major blood vessel was cut, but two of
the lad's fingers were nearly cut off. Eric worked
swiftly and soon had the neck bandaged and the
fingers in splints. He helped the boy to the door and
handed him over to the headman. "Call Mr. Baldwin,"
he directed. "I'll be needing his help."

At once Mr. Baldwin was at the door. He took one
look and opened his mouth to speak: "I say, Hare, . . .
you've got . . ." His voice trailed off, and Eric looked up
in time to see the man's face turn white. He sprang up
to catch Mr. Baldwin as he fell limp into his arms.

Eric called the headman. "This is no good. Put
some cold water on his face, and have the men carry
him to the rest house. I need help. Isn't there someone
who will come and give me a hand?"

After a long moment during which no one moved or
spoke, a little old grandma who spoke Karen said, "I
will help you, Doctor. I'm so old and skinny that the
evil spirits won't bother me." And she really did help,
she on one side of the apparently dead woman, and

Eric on the other.

It was no situation for the fainthearted. The patient's forehead was split open, exposing the tissue underneath. Her cheek was hanging just by the flesh of the lower jaw, leaving a hole through which the teeth and tongue were visible. The flesh of her upper right arm was opened up to the bone on two sides. The left arm had been entirely severed below the elbow. Eric looked to see how this affected his little old helper, but apparently she could handle it. She knew just how to hold and tie and pin up bandages. Eric could feel no heartbeat, but he could see weak spurts of blood at the end of the severed forearm. Perhaps there was a little life, after all.

With tourniquets and bandages Eric and his helper did the best they could to cover the open wounds and to bind severed flesh in place. He then called for some warm milk. When in a few minutes it was brought, he put a spoonful to the woman's lips, and to his surprise she swallowed it. Although apparently dead, the woman swallowed half a cupful of milk, then opened her eyes and spoke faintly, "I am not going to die."

Eric had no doubt; this was a miracle, but if she continued to live she must have surgery much beyond his ability, supplies, and equipment. He urged the headman to get his men to make a bamboo stretcher on which to carry the woman, and to commandeer the largest canoe in the village on which to transport her downstream sixty miles to the nearest government hospital.

With six strong men to paddle it, the canoe bearing the poor woman pushed off at about two-thirty in the morning. As it disappeared in the darkness Eric heard someone running up behind him, and a voice called, "Doctor, Doctor, do you want this?" Eric could not see what the bearer had in his hands, but reached out to take it. It was the cold dead arm that had been hacked off! Eric gasped. "No! No! We can't do anything with that now. Take it away and bury it!"

On his way home Eric stopped at the rest house. Mr. Baldwin was still shaken and pale. He shuddered more when he was told all that had taken place. "I don't see how you can do it," he said with deep conviction. He did not know, of course, how near to fainting Eric had come. But the young missionary knew, and always looked back on that experience as his "graduation" exercise. From that time on he would be a genuine jungle doctor. Many years later he testified that after that gruesome episode, the sight of blood, the most terrible burns, severe mauling by tigers, or goring by buffalo or elephants never again made his head go round and round or made him feel like fainting.

As a new day began to dawn Eric made his way back to his little house. He quickly cleaned up, then rushed over to share the exciting story with the Hamiltons. When Agnes and the nurse returned they too were given the grim details.

News came that the man who had run amok was in jail. The injured woman was still alive, but it was not certain that she could survive. If she did not, the assailant would be hanged. If she lived, he would be sentenced to life imprisonment. With that news the little mission settled back into the usual busy routine.

Six weeks went by. As Eric was treating the usual run of patients, a woman came up to him and gave him a big smile from a face that was scarred and misshapen like nothing he had ever seen. Then she spoke: "Don't you remember me, doctor?"

"No, Auntie," he answered, "I can't recall ever seeing anyone with scars like you have on your face."

With a quick motion the woman threw back the shawl from her left arm, and Eric saw the stump where it had been hacked off. "Now do you know me?" and the woman burst into tears.

Of course Eric knew her then, and remembering the trauma of that night brought an emotional shock. Before he realized what was happening the woman fell at his feet and with her good arm embraced them. Weeping, she cried, "Oh, if you hadn't come that night when the fiend cut me up, I surely would have died. But you weren't afraid of the greased-up men who called you. You weren't afraid of the night or of tigers. You came, and now my son and I both live."

Patients had gathered around. "Aye! Aye!" they said.

"Of course he came! Of course you live. Isn't his name Dr. Rabbit?" asked an old man.

Everyone laughed, including Eric. He wondered what would come next.

"Didn't the rabbit save the elephant's life when the tiger was going to eat him all up?" questioned the old man.

"Aye! Aye!" replied the group.

"And didn't the rabbit tell the horse how to get two sets of teeth so he could whinny?"

"Aye! Aye!" came the chorus.

"And didn't grandfather rabbit overcome grandfather alligator, and pull his tongue out and plant it on the tall tree?"

"Aye! Aye!" The chorus was louder.

"And didn't the rabbit frighten the tiger so that he ran away with the monkey tied on his back, and the jungle bushes were so thick that the monkey's head and arms kept catching in the branches and his stomach was stretched out so much that to this day it is the thinnest part of his body?"

"Aye! Aye!"

"And wasn't the rabbit the best doctor? And didn't his medicine cure every disease?"

"Aye! Aye!"

All at once Eric realized that the old man was referring to the animal folktales of his people. He had already read some of them when studying the Karen language and had noted with satisfaction that the rabbit had superior talents. Still he was surprised at what came next.

"Well, then, isn't this white doctor *our* Dr. Rabbit?"

"Aye! Aye!"

"And won't he overcome all our sickness enemies?"

"Aye! Aye!"

"And won't we all get better if we eat his medicine?"

"Aye! Aye!" and the people nodded and smiled at each other as they said, "Sure, he is *our* Dr. Rabbit. He is *our* Dr. Rabbit!"

It is not difficult to imagine how pleased and satisfied both Eric and Agnes were that evening as they reviewed the happenings of the day and began to realize just how much it meant that they had now become Dr. and Mama Rabbit. Surely this was their "special place."

"Glamour and Glory" of Early Missions

4 "Sonny, what do you want to be when you grow up?" asked a visitor one day, to which the boy replied, "A *returned* missionary."

Perhaps returned missionaries have related experiences and described places and incidents in such a way as to make mission life appear to be invested with an aura of glamour and glory. True, those who have helped to open up new work have felt a kind of joy of living and an excitement in their labors. The plain hard slogging and the challenges and disappointments are often passed over lightly. All will agree that the real glory of missions is in the mysterious and miraculous converting power of God that missionaries have witnessed.

In the story of Dr. Rabbit, of the Burma jungle, we can taste the bittersweet nature of mission life and labor in the early decades of the twentieth century. There is high drama and deep pathos to be found in the volumes of thrilling stories told and written by Dr. Rabbit himself. Eric believed in living life to the full, and his zest for living reveals itself in his lively story style.

From Eric's pen came eleven books with more than two thousand pages of gripping narrative in his inimitable style. Some of his writing is devotional, some inspirational, and some is high adventure that makes it almost impossible to lay the book down once its reading is begun. From 1926 through 1971 he wrote *Jungle Stories; Jungle Heroes, and Other Stories; Clever Queen; Treasure From the Haunted Pagoda; Fullness of Joy; Make God First; An Irish Boy and God; Jungle Storyteller; Fulton's Footprints in Fiji; Dr. Rabbit;* and *Those Juniors.*

More than two hundred articles written by Eric Hare were published in various church journals, besides numerous smaller contributions in specialized departmental publications.

Eric was so much a part of the stories he wrote or told that it is difficult to write his biography without relating those stories. That cannot be done in this book, but a few episodes, vignettes, or anecdotes that help most to tell the story of his life are recounted in the following pages. These are, in the main, drawn from his published works. Some may be verbatim quotations or nearly so.

One day the Hares were delighted to hear Nurse Gibbs say, "Better come with me to visit some of the villages on the other side of the river." The Hares had become familiar with the routine of treating those who came to the dispensary with various tropical disorders and diseases. Now they were excited to be able to visit and observe the people in their home villages.

The missionaries crossed the river in their little motor launch and approached the nearest village. Coming closer, they saw a startled face or two and heard terrified screaming and the cry *"Dawtaka! Dawtaka!"* Miss Gibbs explained that *dawtaka* in jungle superstition was a cross between a devil and a ghost, and that it was supposed to steal babies, fatten them, and then eat them. No wonder the people screamed and ran for their lives if they really thought the white visitors were that kind of evil creatures. Eric and Agnes were to learn more and more how fear dominated the lives of the animist, spirit-worshiping jungle people. If the people were ever to be led to Christ, the Hares just must find a way to take away the inborn fear that controlled the natives' lives.

In the latter part of 1917 the Hamiltons were called to work in Rangoon. The Hares were left in charge of the mission station, and Eric was issued a ministerial license. Now how should they go about carrying out this new responsibility?

As they discussed plans of action Eric concluded, "Agnes dear, don't you think it would work to first start a Sabbath school and then follow up interests with Bible studies? Gradually some would be ready for baptism, and then we could organize a church."

Agnes agreed, but little did the new missionaries yet realize the powerful effect of fear on people's behavior. Eric visited all the villages within ten miles of the mission station. He told the people, "We're going to have Sabbath school at the mission station next Sabbath morning at nine o'clock. Be sure to come, and we will sing you nice songs, show you beautiful pictures, and tell you lovely stories."

"Ugh, ugh," they would grunt agreeably.

Sabbath morning the Hares were excited. Bamboo mats were placed on the floor for folk to sit on, a Picture Roll was hung on the wall, the folding organ was set up, and Eric's trumpet was ready to play. He walked up and down the veranda, waiting for the people—but not a soul came.

So it went for six weeks. It was baffling, but Eric and Agnes tried hard not to become discouraged. Then one Sabbath morning, even before Eric was dressed, he heard someone call from across the river. He looked out to see about two hundred persons on the opposite riverbank, waiting, he was sure, to get across to Sabbath school.

"Agnes, come and see! Here they come, my dear; it

just took some time for them to get the idea, but now look at them!"

Eric and another man rowed the big canoe across to welcome the crowd and to bring them across to Sabbath school, only to be surprised and disappointed to find that the group was on its way to a big devil dance at a village three miles downriver from the mission station.

"Now what will we do?" Eric asked his wife.

"Well," she replied thoughtfully, "if they won't come to our Sabbath school, why don't we take the Sabbath school to them?"

"Excellent idea! That's exactly what we will do."

The next Sabbath, Eric and Agnes set off for the nearest village, armed with trumpet, Picture Roll, and a bag of medicines. As they gave out medicines and applied bandages they said, "When you hear music at the headman's house, . . . come and we'll sing you nice songs and show you beautiful pictures and tell you lovely stories." When at last the music started, the people came—so many, in fact, that the missionaries feared the headman's house would be broken down.

So Sabbath school was held outside. When Eric stopped playing to catch a breath, all the people clapped their hands and cried, "Fine! Fine! Now sing for us." Just what Eric wanted! Now he could sing, then ask, "Did you understand the words?" The people, who had no idea what a religious service was, would say, "No," and he would say, "Then let me explain the words." That would open the way for a simple sermon. So the missionaries sang two hymns, and Eric was reaching for the Picture Roll when the audience began to applaud, and cried, "Fine! Fine! Fine! Now please tell Mama to dance for us!"

Eric and Agnes hardly knew whether to laugh or cry. It really wasn't funny, for they had come to conduct a Sabbath school, and dancing certainly was not on the program. They breathed a quick prayer, God gave them words to say, and they went ahead with the Sabbath school story, while the people listened intently.

Eric later wrote of this first village Sabbath school experience:

"You can only imagine how thrilled we were when we reached home that evening to realize that we had actually held a Sabbath school among the superstitious devil worshipers. By faith we looked forward to the time when many such Sabbath schools would be organized and many of the jungle people would become God's peculiar treasure. As the four of us continued to meet in our own little Sabbath school at the mission station, Nurse Gibbs, Ma Key—a Karen girl who kept house for Miss Gibbs—Mrs. Hare, and I, we prayed that God would mightily bless our feeble efforts, and as we prayed, the good news began to spread far and wide."

As Eric and Agnes understood and loved the Karen people more and more, they were heartened to see a growing response, both to their kindness and compassion in caring for the natives' physical needs and to the simple presentation of the gospel. They saw the dreadful superstition and fear of the devil worshipers dissipate as the people learned to trust the missionaries and then to show faith in the God of the missionaries. The work was slow and sometimes bitterly disappointing, but the Hares believed more and more that they had found their "special place."

A sad note that seems not be mentioned in any of Eric's published works is the loss of their firstborn child. In his notebook journal is this simple entry: "June 5, 1917, Rosalind Agnes Hare born; died June 23. June 24, buried Rosalind Agnes Hare." Their hearts must have been broken, but they would not let this personal loss weaken their faith in the all-wise and loving heavenly Father or deter them from carrying out the ministry to which God had called them.

The story behind the baptism of their first convert is a fascinating one. Elder Hare begins the story in this way:

" 'Did y' hear? Did y' hear? Did y' hear?' called old Rippling Water excitedly as she gathered some old ladies around her in the village of Kawmalay, eight miles from our mission. 'The God worshipers have built a sickness house on the bank of the big river, among the coconut palms. And they say there is a white lady doctor there, and a white man doctor whom they call their Dr. Rabbit, and I'm going down to see them, I am, I am.' "

The unbelieving spirit-worshiping villagers were incredulous. They protested and solemnly warned old Rippling Water that the white people at the sickness house were really *dawtakas.* They would get her to eat some of their strong medicine, and thereafter she would be in their power. They would then eat her and her babies, too.

Old Rippling Water was defiant. "I don't care what you say, I am going down to see them, I am, I am." It didn't matter what they did or said, she was going to see the God worshipers' sickness house. So, taking her 18-year-old daughter, Fair One, she went through rice fields and bamboo forests to the Salween River. A fisherman friend ferried mother and daughter across.

As they approached the dispensary they began to feel afraid. They remembered the warnings. They hid in some bushes to observe what was going on. They saw a mother with a crying baby go into the sickness house. A man with an abcessed hand went in, groaning with pain. Before long the mother came out with a happy, smiling baby in her arms. Then the man came out with his hand neatly bandaged, happiness written on his face.

It was enough for Rippling Water. Taking Fair One by the hand, she said, "Let's go. They are not *dawtakas*. Nobody is being eaten. They go in crying, they come out laughing; they go in sick and come out well." As the two of them came through the door of the dispensary they stood and marveled at what they saw. A white lady doctor was gently caring for an old man with a great sore on his hand. She spoke kind words, and suddenly Rippling Water realized that the nurse was speaking in Karen. The white woman speaks our words," she exclaimed aloud.

"Of course I do, Auntie," Nurse Gibbs said. "How I wish I could come and visit you in your village homes. Then you'd know. But there are so many sick people and so many sick babies coming all day long that I never get a chance to go visiting. Do you know what I need, Auntie? I need a big girl about 18 years old to help me wash bandages and learn how to give babies their castor oil and how to put eye drops in sore eyes."

As they talked on, the lady doctor suddenly noticed Fair One. At once, in the minds of both Nurse Gibbs and Rippling Water, an idea was born. The outcome was that Fair One came to live at the mission station and became the first dispensary assistant. Rippling Water and everyone at the mission station were happy with the arrangement. But back at her village, Fair One's mother ran into sharp criticism and many dire predictions.

Fair One was happy, learned quickly, and became a much-loved and valuable helper. Some months later a young Karen graduate named Thara Peter came from the Meiktila Training School to join the mission staff. With his help they were able to start a small but successful school.

Just when the future was looking very bright, Nurse Gibbs went on furlough and the Hamiltons were called to pastoral duties in Rangoon. Now Dr. Rabbit and Mama Rabbit, Thara Peter, and Fair One had to care for the dispensary, school, and all. It was a difficult challenge, but they knew that God was with them, for now they were beginning to see the fruitage of their labor.

One day Fair One said to Eric, "Dr. Rabbit, I've been here more than two years now. I've learned to work and I've learned to read. Every day I read part of the Golden Book. In that Book I've found Jesus, and I believe He is the Son of God. Doctor, I would like to be baptized and become a God worshiper too."

Eric was too choked up with happiness to speak for a few moments. "I'm so glad, Fair One. Next time your mother comes down we will ask her what she thinks of it."

In a few days Rippling Water came, and her reaction was "Well, I don't mind if she does become a God worshiper. We have worshiped the devils and the evil spirits all our lives, and they are no good. And, Doctor, I'll tell you what—maybe when I know a little more I might become a God worshiper too."

The little mission family could not have been happier when the day came for the first convert among the Karens at Ohn Dow to be baptized. Pastor A. H. Williams was called to perform the sacred rite. He had been with Pastor Hamilton when the site for the mission had been selected, so it was a high day for him, as well.

When news of Fair One's baptism reached her village, the villagers reacted by having a curse put on Rippling Water's house, and she was driven from their midst with sticks and stones. She first took refuge at the mission, then with friends.

The cursed house now gave forth terrifying screams, groans, and yells. The troubled villagers decided to burn it, but no one brave enough to light a match could be found. "Let's pull it down," they said, but no one would dare to touch it. Finally they decided to make Rippling Water pull down her house. The poor woman came weeping to Eric. "How can I pull a house down? I'm only a little old woman. How I wish I could sell the old house. I'd be glad to live somewhere else."

At once Eric thought of two hundred rupees the mission had received with which to build a boys' home at their growing school. Rippling Water was glad to sell her house for fifty rupees, and Eric and the bigger schoolboys would be able to pull the house apart and transport the best of the materials to the school. Eric got permission from the village council to buy and transfer the house. The village people were glad to get rid of the cursed house, not caring what the devils might do to the God worshipers.

The materials in Rippling Water's house were found to be sound. In a short time the house was dismantled and the materials carried on bullock wagons to the riverbank opposite the mission station. All the boards and posts were tied together to form a big raft and were towed across the river by the motor launch. Three weeks later the house was all assembled, and the boys had a new home. Now instead of the screaming of evil spirits, gospel songs were heard from the once-haunted house of Rippling Water.

The little mission staff sang a doxology, for in a short time not only was the house "converted," but within a few months a brother and a sister of Fair One were baptized, and a little later the mother, old Rippling Water herself.

Thara Pa-Deh, Dr. Rabbit, was not above adding a bit of showmanship to reinforce his efforts to gain public confidence. When he learned that in Karen folklore the rabbit was credited with superior wisdom and ability, he had readily agreed to be called Dr. Rabbit. He designed labels for the various substances used in simple jungle medicine, all with a small drawing of a rabbit and called Bunny Brand. Sales of dispensary medicines began to grow rapidly.

On another occasion Eric added a dramatic touch in applied psychology. In his book *Treasure From the Haunted Pagoda* he tells what happened:

" 'Doctor, Doctor,' called the chief fisherman from Kawkeyet as he came down the trail with seventeen of his servants, 'I've got a tooth that I want pulled out,' and as I looked up I caught the picture of a man who expected to have a big operation and had brought his seventeen servants to assist. Always willing to oblige, and having pulled hundreds of teeth since the first one fell out with the vibrations, I decided not to disappoint him, and welcomed him as one chief would welcome another. I brought him in, gave him my best mat, then stood his seventeen servants all around the room. To one I gave a towel, to another the absorbent cotton, to another a bundle of bamboo swab sticks. Another held a glass of water, another the permanganate crystals. Still others held the oil of cloves and the lance and the forceps on trays a little farther down the line until every man had something to hold.

"I then took up my position in front of my patient and called for the man with the cotton and the man with the sticks to step forward. I made a swab very carefully and then called for the oil of cloves. That man stepped forward, and dipping the swab, I painted the tooth with oil of cloves.

" 'That's hot, isn't it, Uncle?' I said.

"He nodded. I then put a few permanganate crystals in the glass of water, asked the man with the towel to stand at the right and the man with the basin to stand at the left, had the man with the forceps step forward, then took them with a flourish and fastened them on the tooth. It was so loose I could have pulled it with my fingers, but that would never have done.

"I was just about to pull the tooth when the dear old man suddenly found out that the oil of cloves had taken the pain from his tooth. He thereupon decided not to have the tooth pulled that day, but instead to buy a bottle of this hot medicine and paint his tooth with that. Quickly lifting his hands, he caught mine to stop me from pulling till he could explain, but the tooth was so loose that the jerk pulled it right out.

"I gave it to the man with the towel and, while the permanganate water and the basin were serving their purposes, told him to dry the tooth in the sun, tie a string around it, and hang it behind the door to remind him always of the Ohn Daw dispensary. That man went everywhere saying that the jungle doctor at Ohn Daw was the greatest dentist that ever walked the earth."

Dr. and Mama Rabbit witnessed steady growth in the Ohn Daw mission. The school that began in May, 1919, with Thara Peter in charge of ten pupils, opened two years later with sixty-three pupils and three teachers. The Hare family grew as well, with the birth of Eileen Nita, July 19, 1918. In October of that year, in answer to an earnest plea by Dr. Rabbit, a Karen evangelist by the name of Tha Myaing was added to the staff.

Eric was greatly encouraged as it became apparent that the influence of the dispensary and school at Ohn Daw was spreading farther and farther out into the jungle villages. Young men and women who were eager to learn and to improve their lives were attracted to the school. It was not long before eight fine young men were baptized, rejoicing to have been delivered from a life of superstition and fear. They were the firstfruits of the mission school.

One of these, Ohn Bwint, although he had not completed the prescribed training to be a teacher, answered the request of Hte Po, headman of the village of La Po Ta, some eighteen miles from the mission station, and began to teach in that village. In that way an outstation was established, the first of many. Ohn Bwint taught well and witnessed to his faith zealously. At the end of the school year he came to the little mission camp meeting with five bullock wagons loaded with people. Hte Po, village headman, was ready for baptism.

It was great to have three teachers in the school and an evangelist added to the staff. But the dispensary load increased daily, and the oversight of all the misson activities made it imperative to add an associate missionary. In that way one or the other of the missionaries could be in the field regularly. Eric's plea for an associate finally was answered, and in December, 1920, Harold Baird arrived. Harold was a graduate nurse from Sydney Sanitarium in Australia. He was also a trumpet player, which rated high on the scale with Dr. Rabbit. Harold's fiancée was soon to graduate from the nurse's course and would join them at the Ohn Daw mission. Eric and Agnes were delighted.

In the Karen language there are no final consonants. To pronounce Baird's name, the people would have to say, "Bair-da," or leave off the *d* to make it sound like "Bair." Spelling made no difference in sound, so Dr. Rabbit's new associate became Dr. Bear. The jungle folk were delighted with that coincidence, and they were pleased with the man.

As Dr. Bear faced up to the raw realities of jungle life, Eric relived his initiation into the nerve-racking and sometimes heartbreaking practice of jungle medicine. Harold learned quickly and became skillful in performing lifesaving surgery, including amputations. The skill of Dr. Bear spread far and wide. Among many stories of his success as a jungle doctor is a classic involving a patient too large to pass through the dispensary door.

A "lady" elephant was brought to the dispensary with a great swelling wound, terribly infected. Dr. Bear ingeniously cleansed and dressed the deep wound and asked that the suffering beast be brought back in the morning for further treatment under the same big tree. This time the elephant lay down on first command and was treated, and the owner was asked to bring her again in the morning. Next morning the owner was shocked to find the elephant gone. He looked here and there and finally discovered the patient lying in the proper spot to receive treatment. Further, Eric vouched for the fact that for six weeks the elephant came by herself to receive treatment.

By then the wound had healed. The owner mounted the lady patient's head and said to her, "We're going away now. Say Salaam to the doctors." The elephant went down on her knees and saluted with her trunk. Eric decided she should have a going-away present and gave her a small loaf of bread. Incredibly, Dr. Rabbit and Dr. Bear saw tears run out of the elephant's eyes and down over her cheeks. The missionaries felt some unusual moisture in their own eyes.

A year after Dr. Bear came to Ohn Daw, another notable arrival was announced on December 5, 1921, when to Mama and Dr. Rabbit, Leonard Newlon Hare was born. A few months later, in August of 1922, Eric and Agnes went on furlough to Australia by way of Singapore, happy that they could show off their offspring to Father and Mother Fulton and other relatives and friends. But Eric had an additional goal, a special mission to work at while on furlough.

Shortly before their furlough began, Eric went on a preaching tour, taking Harold Baird and fifteen boys from the school. The students helped carry supplies and equipment, but also learned to be preachers and evangelists. Eric took his cornet, which had worked to get attention on previous tours. Harold took his cornet too. When L. W. Melendy, the union mission secretary, learned of the proposed itinerary, he begged to go along with them, rather than take his scheduled vacation-hill leave. And he also played a cornet!

The music of three cornets brought the people together in a way that seemed miraculous. The village of Parkati seemed deserted when the mission party arrived, but the three instruments began their rousing rendition of "Lift Up the Trumpet, and Loud Let it Ring." As Eric described it:

"From out of the bamboo jungle they came—running, laughing, carrying their little ones on their backs—mothers and fathers, uncles and aunties, grandpas and grandmas, and all the little cousins. Till at last there were more than fifty at our meeting! No wonder Tha Myaing had a big smile on his face when he got up to preach! And no wonder the boys danced up and down and clapped their hands after the meeting and said, 'We know what did it! It was the trumpets! It was the trumpets!' Then looking very much in earnest, they added, 'Wouldn't it be wonderful if everyone of us had a trumpet!' "

Then and there the dream was born to have a jungle band. By the time their tour ended, Eric had formed his plan. Soon he and his family would go on furlough and he would go from church to church and school to school and camp meeting to camp meeting to tell about his work in Burma. You may be sure it was exciting when he described the preaching tours with the mission staff and with the big boys who were learning to preach, and their eagerness for each to have an instrument to help preach the gospel.

Eric's appeals were so interesting and so earnest, and the generosity of the Australian members was so great, that much before the furlough ended, Eric had

collected twenty-three silver and brass instruments.
They weren't all cornets and trumpets, either; they
were an assortment sufficient to round out a band
with all the essential instrumental voices. A jubilant
missionary broke into verse in this way:

"We packed them in boxes—
　ironbound boxes—
And took them to Burma,
　a long way from home,
To the boys in the jungle
　who wanted some trumpets,
To help preach the gospel
　where'er they might roam."

In October of 1923 the Hares returned to Kamamaung with their personal things and those "ironbound boxes." A week went by as Eric and Agnes
settled back into the routine of the mission station.
The boys at the school were consumed with curiosity
and tried to figure out what was in those boxes.

Then one morning in chapel Eric read the names of
the boys who had been chosen to play in the band. The
first band practice was set for noon that day, but it
wasn't possible for anyone to wait until noon. Ample
help was on the spot to pry the covers off the boxes.

One by one the instruments were handed to those
who had been chosen. They had seen trumpets, of
course, but here were silver and brass instruments
they had never seen. One can only imagine how
clumsy were their attempts to take hold of an
instrument, to learn how to place and move their
fingers, how to place their lips, and how even to make
a sound. And when they did succeed in making
sounds, what a horrible din followed! It was so bad
that Agnes had to flee into the jungle with the baby to
avoid going insane—or so she said. Eric was so
exhausted after three hours of that kind of band

practice that he succumbed to a severe attack of malaria. But the tooting went on, morning, noon, and night, until Eric was tempted to think he had made a grave mistake. How could they ever function as a band when not one of the boys could make the same sound twice in succession?

The boys themselves found the solution. They were so eager to "play the band" to help carry the gospel to their people that they made it the subject of constant prayer. Eric reported the outcome in these words: "The great God whom we love and serve, the God who has given white men wisdom enough to make these marvelous instruments, gave those humble jungle boys enough skill to play them. It sounds like a fairy tale, but just exactly four weeks from our first band practice, we were holding our first open-air meeting in a village nearby. Why, no, we didn't play any difficult music. We played three little hymn tunes, but we played them again and again, and the jungle people said it was wonderful, and I think it was wonderful too."

The band brought a new day for Burma evangelism. Practice brought great improvement and many opportunities to give a strong Christian witness followed. To the missionaries, the band's significant accomplishment was to put to rest the unreasoning fear the villagers had of *dawtakas* and other evil spirits. When the band played, the people lost their fears. The band played for annual meetings at outstations, and was very popular at camp meetings, which grew in attendance from thirty the first year to 1,500 in a very short time. Thus it was through medical attention, education, evangelism, and music that the confidence and love of the Karen people were won and the number of believers steadily increased. Satan fought for every inch of territory, using a variety of troubles to discourage the missionaries, but they found that for every one of the few major crises and many minor ones, God had a special miracle to match.

Life flowed on for the missionaries at Ohn Daw station. Every day brought happenings that would provide intriguing plots and thrilling drama for countless stories. You may be sure Eric B. Hare made the most of them.

In March, 1926, Eric sailed from Rangoon, bound eventually for a General Conference session in Milwaukee, Wisconsin. Agnes remained in their jungle home with the children. Eric's travel route took him to several points in Asia and Europe, where he visited briefly with relatives and friends.

Meetings of the General Conference session ran from May 27 to June 14. Before sailing from San Francisco on August 17, Eric attended and took part in two California camp meetings and was able to visit relatives in the Bay Area.

Elder Hare arrived in Burma on September 30 after a brief stop in Singapore, where he visited his sister Nettie Johanson and her husband, Eric. He was grateful to find all was well. The routine care of the dispensary and the school, and some field work, kept the Hare family busy from September of 1926 to January of 1930. Their duties may have been routine, but the time was not uneventful. For a month, early in 1927, Eric was away attending a committee meeting in Poona, India. In March of that year, their daughter Eileen began to attend school at Vincent Hill, Mussoorie, India, returning home in January, 1929.

A tragic event of those years was the severe attack of meningitis that caused little Verna May to lose her hearing. Born May 2, 1929, she became deaf in January, 1930. A price like this is often paid by the self-sacrificing trailblazers who open up the work of the church in new areas.

On their second furlough, the Eric Hare family

made brief visits with family members and friends in Singapore, Australia, New Zealand, and later in the West and Northwest of the United States. Again Eric took part in several camp meetings along the West Coast. On November 1, 1930, the Hares boarded the S.S. *President Coolidge,* and arrived in Rangoon on December 10.

What joy to see the mission work expanding rapidly as more and more Karen youth were educated and trained to be medical workers, teachers, preachers, and leaders. Then, April 14, 1933, brought special delight, when Peter Edgar Hare was born.

Everything at the mission grew surprisingly, in spite of problems common in developing work. One major concern was the deafness of Verna May. Reluctantly they decided to request a transfer to California, where they would be near to competent help for Verna May's hearing problem.

The Hare family arrived in Oakland, California, May 30, 1934. Almost immediately Eric began a new assignment as secretary of the missionary volunteer and Sabbath school departments of the Northern California Conference. For him it was a kind of sabbatical leave, seven years away from their beloved Burma.

Verna May was enrolled in the Hawthorn Oral School for the Deaf. The family attended the 1936 session of the General Conference. Eileen went to Lodi, California, to attend the Adventist academy there, graduating in May, 1937, and enrolling a short time later at Pacific Union College. In September of that year, Leonard enrolled at Lodi Academy, graduating in May, 1940, as president of his class. On the 14th of May that year, daughter Eileen was married to Ivan Higgins, having been employed since her graduation from PUC as an office secretary in the Northern California Conference office. Leonard went to Pacific

Union College in August to begin his college work. In that same month Eric accepted a call to serve as Sabbath school department secretary in the Southern California Conference. The Hares located in Glendale, California, and Verna May began to attend school there. Near the end of 1940 Eileen and Ivan sailed to India to begin their mission service.

In March, 1941, Eric was delighted to accept a call to return to Burma to serve as secretary of three departments in the Burma Union office: Sabbath school, missionary volunteer, and home missionary. He still felt that Burma, among the Karens, was his "special place," although now his duties would be in a much wider scope. He accepted at once, but it was October before the Hares reached Burma.

At once they swung into action. Eric was invited to conduct a Week of Prayer series at the Meiktila Training School, December 4-11. He enjoyed this time with the students very much, but he could not then know that this exercise would be almost the last of its kind to be performed in what we would call "normal" times. Life would never again be the same for Burma and for many other countries. On December 7, 1941, Japan declared war on England and the United States and struck devastating blows at Pearl Harbor, Hong Kong, and Manila.

The Hare Trumpet Trio, with son Peter and grandson Calvin.

The Jungle Band, at Ohn Daw School.

The Hare family in 1934.

"Dr. Rabbit" at the Ohn Daw Dispensary.

A Sabbath school workshop in Baghdad, Iraq.

A blind camper tries out the Hare trumpet.

Preview of the End

5 of the World

For many months international tension had been building. Early in 1937 ugly rumors came from the Far East, arousing suspicions and fears. Then on July 7, 1937, Japan invaded China in earnest, their troops marching toward Peking and Shanghai. Two years later, real alarm began to be felt in the West as unsettled conditions culminated in the invasion of Poland by Germany, beginning September 1, 1939. From then on, the uneasy feelings were shared by everyone almost everywhere as the news media reported wars and rumors of wars in many places. In Burma, however, all seemed peaceful and quiet for a time. But thoughts of peace and safety faded fast with the news that on December 7, 1941, Japan suddenly and viciously attacked the United States naval forces and installations at Pearl Harbor, Hawaii. It was an eruption that sent shock waves in all directions.

The very next day the United States of America declared war on Japan. Three days after declaring war on Japan, she declared war on Germany and Italy. The day after the Pearl Harbor attack, Great Britain declared war on Japan. Burma, being a British protectorate, was immediately involved. Thus, on December 13, Japanese planes flew over Rangoon. Ten days later the first of ninety-two air raids on the Rangoon area took place. On that first attack, between fifty and sixty planes unloaded bombs on East

Rangoon and the shipping facilities. Casualties numbered in the thousands.

It was logical that Japan should concentrate its attacks on Rangoon. Aside from being the nation's capital, it was a shipping point for supplies destined for the famous Burma Road. The Burma Road had become a vital lifeline to China. A good motor road and railway ran from Rangoon to Lashio, 620 miles away. From Lashio the Burma Road ran about seven hundred crooked, hilly miles across the border to Kunming. In the city of Rangoon, factories were working in haste to assemble thirty thousand trucks. Each day two hundred or more trucks rolled off the assembly line to be loaded with ammunition and other war materials and sent off to China over the Burma Road. This made Rangoon a prime target for Japanese bombs. It was clear that the enemy would not rest until that strategic door to China was closed.

Eric B. Hare was on the scene, and with his penchant for keeping meticulous records of events and for registering emotions, he provided a saga of great human interest. From December 4 to 11 he was at the Meiktila Training School to conduct Week of Prayer services. During those few days World War II began. In a notebook diary Eric chronicled an almost daily account of enemy attacks and what his family and those of other expatriates did as they were forced to evacuate. More than one hundred entries provide a narrative outline of events that would seem to justify the title of this chapter, "Preview of the End of the World."

On December 13, members in Rangoon were in church when the first air raid took place. No bombs were dropped, but the sight of enemy planes caused fear and panic among the inhabitants, and evacuation began immediately. On foot or using every conceivable conveyance, the people fled in terror.

The next day was quiet. No enemy planes appeared. A mysterious woman's voice from Tokyo kept broadcasting warnings for the people to leave the city. When three or four days of quiet followed, Eric decided to carry on according to plan with a week of special meetings at his old mission station in Kamamaung. By the time a week had passed with no further attacks, evacuation of Rangoon stopped, and some people returned.

Eric finished his meetings at the mission station, and with Peter, the mission superintendent, he was on his way back down the Salween River when the second air raid came. They first heard a great roar, then looked up to see fifteen enemy planes in one formation and twenty-seven in another headed directly for Rangoon.

With a shock Eric realized what was happening. Those planes with their lethal freight were on their way to the city where his home and family were. What would happen to them? It was the next morning before Eric and Peter reached Rangoon. They found homes and families intact, but these loved ones had a vivid and exciting story to tell. Let's allow Eric to recount it in his own words:

"As the siren wailed its warning, they scrambled into a big cement gutter about four feet deep and two feet wide, running at the back of our house. At ten-thirty, straight from the east, riding on the beams of the rising sun, came fifty-one enemy planes. And soon, seemingly right overhead, they saw the 'yellow bellies,' as everyone called them, dropping their 'eggs.' The next instant they saw our 'flying tigers' giving them battle in their P-40's. They saw the machine-gunning. They saw the great clouds of smoke. They saw the leaping tongues of fire and heard the screaming, the crying, the yelling, the shouting, of the thousands who were fleeing from the destruction.

They saw three enemy planes shot out of the air. They saw the Japanese pilots bail out in their parachutes. One chute failed to open, and we learned afterward that that pilot dropped right into the cemetery. Two others, landing in the city and finding themselves surrounded by policemen and about to be arrested, committed hara-kiri; that is, they ripped open their abdomens and bled to death. As another one floated down, he began machine-gunning the women and children who were looking on. One of our pillboxes nearby replied in the same language and literally sawed off his dangling legs in midair and tore his chute to ribbons so that his legless body fell to its death on the pavement below."

Such was the gruesome introduction to the grim realities of war as it came to the land of the golden pagodas. Tragedy for a great number of Rangoon residents might have been avoided had they obeyed instructions to go immediately to trenches or other shelters at the first sounding of the warning sirens. But the dogfights between airplanes above the city were so fascinating that thousands stood in the streets to watch, disregarding the warnings. It was reported that 1,350 civilians met sudden death in the streets in that one air raid, and at least twice that number were wounded and taken to hospitals. That was on object lesson too clear to be missed.

The fourth enemy attack on Rangoon came about midmorning on Christmas Day. The wail of sirens brought an abrupt end to thoughts of a quiet Christmas dinner together in the home. Instead, all the Hares crouched in the gutter and watched Allied planes roar off to intercept seventy-five enemy planes. In the next half hour, twenty-one of the invader planes were shot down. However, four attackers slipped through and rained down 111 incendiary bombs on the city. The Hares saw and heard once more the devastating results.

A major Burma mission project at that time was to load sixteen large trucks with medical and mission supplies for the Adventist Inland China missions. Now, to help meet the immediate dire emergency, Mr. Coberly, the project director, put one of these trucks at the disposal of Dr. Walker from the Seventh-day Adventist clinic, and others from the union office, with which to improvise an ambulance unit. As soon as the explosions ceased, the men rushed off to see what assistance they might give. The devastation and carnage they saw was beyond adequate description. The air-raid warden directed them to a certain section that had been hit hard. In about two and one-half hours they picked up seventeen persons who were still living and took them to a hospital. Eric could never forget the shock and shudder he felt when he stumbled over a human head rolling in the dust, and when he picked up a severed leg.

Coberly's convoy to China might be able to leave at any moment, so rather than Eric and others helping as an independent unit, it was decided that they would join civil-defense workers. Eric began then to serve as a St. John's (similar to the Red Cross) ambulance driver. He was privileged to work in that capacity until the last day of Rangoon's freedom, when all foreign civilians were evacuated.

The actual invasion of Burma came early in January, 1942, at two places on the southern and southeastern borders. The American consul urged the expatriate workers to get their women and children out to India. That seemed to be wise, so the men went at once to shipping offices to book passage for the twelve women and fifteen children. The agent said, "We haven't had any kind of ship for two weeks, and we don't know when, if ever, we'll get another one. We have three thousand names on our waiting list, but it won't hurt to add a few more."

The prospect looked hopeless, but the missionaries were sustained by God's promises to provide a sanctuary for them in an alien land or to make a way of escape. They could only get the women and children ready and pray and wait.

On January 19, the twenty-seventh, twenty-eighth, and twenty-ninth air raids hit Rangoon. The next day the telephone rang and the American consul announced, "We have a little freighter going to Calcutta. It has just unloaded some tanks and bombs. It isn't listed with the steamship agents. If you can get some of your women and children to the wharf by 3:00 P.M., we'll take them across for you."

Just an hour and a half to ready bedrolls and pack suitcases! One of Mr. Coberly's China trucks was available for transport to the ship, and at the appointed hour the first group of evacuee women and children went aboard and soon were safely away. Missionaries of other denominations were aboard as well, some having fled overland from Bangkok.

Two days later the missionary men in Rangoon heard the staggering news that a ship making the Rangoon-Calcutta run had been torpedoed and sunk by enemy submarines. A couple days after that, another boat was sunk, but passengers and crew came ashore on the southern coast of Burma in lifeboats and on rafts. Anxiety mounted as the men waited for word about their women and children, but the men refused to give up hope.

What a thrill, about a week later, to receive an airmail letter from Agnes Hare, in which she said, "As our little freighter sailed out of the Rangoon River into the Bay of Bengal, a thick, heavy fog settled down around us, and we couldn't see the sun for four days. Not until we were in the Hooghly River, on our way up to Calcutta, did the sun shine again. Then, when we landed and bought the first newspaper, we read that two boats had been torpedoed and sunk while we were *covered with the cloud.*"

Back in Rangoon more transportation was found, so by February 3 the last of the expatriot women and children were safely off to Calcutta. For three weeks enemy forces had been advancing from the border crossings toward Rangoon, so when Mr. Coberly got back from taking the last of the women and children to the ship in his truck, everyone felt like celebrating. The mission workers shook his hand and thanked him heartily. His response was a surprise: "Goodbye, gentlemen!"

Eric replied, "Come now, Coberly, we're just beginning to like you, and you're going off to leave us now?"

Coberly replied, "Gentlemen, it's *strange,* to say the least, but you know my sixteen trucks have been practically all loaded for six weeks. I've just been waiting for my final clearance papers from the customhouse. Every day I go around. Every day they shake their heads and say, 'Not finished yet, Mr. Coberly, not finished yet. Come tomorrow.' Now, almost from habit I called in at the customs office on my way home from the wharf after taking the *last* of your women and children to the boat, and as I entered the door the clerk smiled and said, 'All finished, Mr. Coberly, all finished. Here you are. You can leave anytime.' So now we're all ready to go. We'll be starting off as the moon comes up tonight, God willing and siren permitting."

More than a happenstance, thought Eric. He thought, too, of the bravery and dedication of young men and women who under the most forbidding circumstances were headed for the remote and lonely interior of China. At the Burma hill station of Kalaw, five young missionaries had just completed a year of

Chinese language study. The young men had sent their wives on to China by plane, and now each was ready to take the wheel of one of Mr. Coberly's trucks to drive it over the Burma Road.

The men left behind knew that they and the church in Burma had come to a time of great affliction and peril. Thara Peter and his faithful church members in Ohn Daw were right in the path of invading forces streaming across the border from Siam. There was no way to communicate with Ohn Daw. The only resort was to prayer, to which the men in Rangoon came constantly, by faith believing that God would use these terrible experiences to refine and purify His peculiar treasure.

The intensity and frequency of the bombing increased until on the Sabbath following the departure of the missionary women and children there were eight bombing runs, beginning at two-thirty in the morning. The remainder of the night was spent in the gutters. It was extremely uncomfortable, and it was terrifying.

Just before dawn, five waves of enemy bombers passed directly overhead at low altitude and were met by antiaircraft fire. Bombs dropped and the yellow bellies droned away to the north of the great pagoda, pursued by the defending night fighters. It was an exciting but deadly grim fireworks display.

At 6:30 A.M. Eric crawled out of the gutter, feeling numb and most uncomfortable in spite of the excitement of the night. He remembered that it was Sabbath and soon would be time for Sabbath school. But surely no one would come, he thought. The church members had spent most of the night in the gutters. How could they be expected to come? Of course, Eric would not miss Sabbath school for anything. He dressed and walked to church. When the superintendent stood to greet the members, thirty-seven of their 150 members were present. When the roll was called they were amazed to find that everyone who was absent had been evacuated to Calcutta, Mandalay, or Bassein, or to some country place.

Those faithful members present that morning would never forget the opening song, "A Shelter in the Time of Storm." Never had that song been sung with more feeling. The stories those members related and the testimonies they gave of miracles of providential guidance and care were gloriously thrilling. No wonder they sang with such fervor!

Summing up the impressions on that occasion, Eric wrote, "It is true! The fires of trouble and affliction do make the treasure shine brighter!"

By February 11 it became clear that the fate of Rangoon had been sealed. All natural barriers had now been crossed by the invaders, which meant that it would be only a matter of days until all of Burma would be in enemy hands.

The missionary men now devoted full-time to help church members evacuate, taking them to trains or riverboats. In between times they concentrated on one suitcase apiece for their personal things, the limit because the only means of escape for them was by Pastor Christensen's car. Could four men with one suitcase and a small bundle of rugs each, plus gasoline for the trip, possibly fit into one small car? They had to try. But, oh, the trauma of choosing what to leave behind! Eric's own poignant words tell the story:

"What an ordeal! If sudden destruction snatched from you every worldly possession, I think it would be easier to say, 'Thy will be done,' and praise God for preserving your life than to sit down and coolly choose from your priceless possessions only what you could put into one suitcase.

" 'You had better store your boxes in the mission

house,' advised Pastor Meleen, our superintendent. 'There is no hope once the bandits and looters start work, but we will always feel we did our best if we store them all here.'

"So I packed up my boxes, the boxes that we had brought to Burma just four months before, our pictures, our photos, our linen, Mrs. Hare's darling dishes, our sweeper, our stand lamp. The weight in my heart and the lump in my throat grew heavier and bigger with each moment, and as I shut the lid on little Peter's tin train and Verna May's baby doll, I felt as though I had conducted a funeral. I felt like the undertaker, the preacher, the mourners, all in one. There were still three boxes that had not been unpacked yet. I might as well have a grand funeral while I was about it. I wanted to take one last, loving glance. My hand trembled as I lifted the lid. There they lay, so beautiful and bright, seven new brass band instruments, given by friends and loved ones in America and Australia for my famous jungle band. There was the E-flat tuba that had never been played yet. There lay the euphonium, the two trombones, and the three silver-plated cornets. What sacrifice they represented. What possibilities! But it was too painful. I closed the box quickly and turned to peep into the others. My books, the cream of my library. My music, a collection of band music, choir music, and quartet music, and my file, a lifelong collection of clippings: a story, a poem, a gem for every occasion! How could I part with it all! My throat choked, my tears fell. I closed the boxes quickly, . . . called a cartman, and lovingly and tenderly interred them in the mission house."

A neighbor woman came to tell Eric that with her brother and his family she was planning to go by land route to India. They could take with them just one suitcase and one bed bundle each. She could not take her car, could not sell it, and could not bear to leave it for the enemy to use. They would have to leave everything else in the house. She begged Eric to take her car. "Use it as long as you can. But if you ever have to abandon it, you take a gallon of gasoline and pour over it and set it afire."

As the poor woman turned quickly to hide her grief, Eric stood, dazed and hardly able to believe that now there would be two cars for four men. There would be room to pack in a few more valuables.

The next day Dr. and Mrs. Walker, Pastor Sargent, and Pastor Johanson came to the mission house with news that Singapore had fallen to the enemy. At the Irrawaddy Delta Mission, where Pastors Sargent and Johanson had been serving, the delta Burmese were so openly hostile that the commissioner had ordered the missionaries to leave. The four of them planned to go by riverboat, country sail boat, and train to Calcutta.

When they departed in the morning they left their car for the evacuation group to use. Now the Rangoon men could take not only a few more personal things but also the most essential office records. It even allowed them to indulge the hope that the mission headquarters might be established at Maymyo in northern Burma.

The climax for Rangoon came quickly. On February 17 the enemy forces crossed the Bilin River, within eighty miles of the city. Pastor Christensen worked untiringly to help the few remaining church members to get away. As Eric went on ambulance duty the next day he found that the St. John's ambulance crew had been dismissed and everyone instructed to leave the city. Eric offered to stay on duty with the chief until morning, as it would be impossible to leave that night. In the morning he stopped at a corner to get a newspaper, hoping to get more information, but no paperboy showed up. An Indian workman told Eric that the newspaper workers had been given two months' pay and told to go *jildy,* which means "very quickly." As Eric took in the situation he knew it was time for him and his companions to go *jildy.*

The men at the mission office tried to call the consul to make sure they were not leaving before it was really necessary. The telephone office was closed, and when Mr. Meleen drove to the consul's office he found it closed. As the day passed the men learned that the military headquarters had moved out, as had government headquarters and the post offices. Merchants and bankers had all cleared out. Even the hospitals had dismissed their employees. By evening, traffic was in a hopeless tangle of cars, trucks, and busses, and at every service station there were riot conditions as people fought for the last available drops of gasoline in the city.

The mission office boys were dismissed, and the church pastor worked to get the two remaining church families out on a riverboat. There were far too many waiting to leave on the boat, so they were disappointed. Another way seemed to open up, but even after the two families were on board, the military took over the boat for that day, and all civilians had to disembark.

The trauma of that experience reminded Eric of the Bible description of those who wait until summer is ended and the harvest is past, and then wail, "Too late! Too late! We are not saved." "I've heard it," he later wrote.

"Have you ever read of the weeping and wailing and gnashing of teeth? I've seen it, and it is the most painful sight that human eyes could see and the most awful sound that human ears could hear."

Late in the day Mr. Baldwin came with the news that the military had taken over the trains but that

two evacuee trains north and two west would run the
next day. They would have to get the two families to
the station and through the gates, and then they
could be on their way. That was good news. Then Mr.
Baldwin showed them a poster he had picked up. It
read: "Civilians of Rangoon are hereby given forty-
eight hours' notice to get out of the city. Forty-eight
hours from now the city will be closed, and all vehicles
found therein after that period of time will be
destroyed. By order, Commissioner of Police."

Eric and his companions felt for a moment that the
dogs of doom were nipping at their heels, but there
might still be one chance. If they could get the last two
families to the station that evening, they might get
aboard the train the next morning, and the missionaries could make their escape in time.

As they approached the central railway station
they were not prepared for the sight that met their
eyes. The station with its gardens, lawns, sidewalks,
and parking areas, ordinarily acres and acres of
well-kept neatness and beauty, was covered with the
reclining forms of thousands of Indians and Chinese
hoping to board the train in the morning. Soldiers
guarded the gates with fixed bayonets.

Eric prayed as he had never prayed before as he led
the little group single file, stepping over and around
prone forms. They had no authority, passes, tickets,
or permits. But Eric and Mr. Baldwin were wearing
their ambulance uniforms, which a British guard
recognized, and he asked his buddy on the other side
of the gate to open up and let them through. A little
later Mr. Baldwin brought the office boys in, and the
gate was opened for them, too. The remainder of the
night was spent praising God.

Sabbath, February 21, 1942, would long be
remembered by those who were in Rangoon that day.
Eric rose early, made his bed, and patted it goodbye.

He went into the kitchen and bade a tearful goodbye to the new kerosene range, just brought from America, to the refrigerator, the rugs, pictures, and chairs; then he turned the key in the door and cried, "Goodbye, home sweet home."

Hurrying to the mission house, Eric found the other three men finishing their packing, suffering in silence. The cars were loaded, they were ready to go. They entered the church for the last time, with aching but subdued hearts, to sing a final song:

"When through fiery trials thy pathway shall lie,
 My grace all sufficient shall be thy supply;
 The flame shall not hurt thee; I only design
 Thy dross to consume and thy gold to refine.

"The soul that on Jesus doth lean for repose,
 I will not, I will not desert to his foes;
 That soul, though all hell should endeavor to shake,
 I'll never, no, never, no, never forsake."

Later Eric described the scene: "The preacher prayed his last prayer. The Bible was closed on the altar, and with pews all emptied of men, we closed the door."

Silent and tearful, they opened the gates, about to drive out to join the endless procession of refugees, when the ninety-second air raid siren sounded. An awful battle raged overhead, but the fleeing people jamming the streets on foot, cycling, or riding in rickshas, gharries, carts, or cars gave little heed. As the missionaries waited for the all-clear signal they saw small groups of people walking into the city. Many of them had short hair and were dressed alike. Inquiry brought them information that as the city was being abandoned, the wardens at the insane asylum freed the inmates to go where they would. Prison wardens gave the prisoners a new outfit of clothing each and turned them loose. Three thousand criminals were allowed to walk into town. Surely, Eric thought, we have come to evil days.

Time seemed endless before the all clear sounded. With heavy hearts and without speaking, the missionaries in their cars eased out into the great procession of sad and homeless refugees fleeing the doomed city. It was a scene to make good angels weep, and it was certain that evil spirits gloated over what they saw. It was a time for unquestioning faith in an overruling providence.

Eric and his three companions could not know what lay ahead for them, but already they had seen enough to know for a certainty that God honors the exercise of faith, making a way for His faithful ones when there seems to be no way. They had already witnessed enough to feel that they were participating in at least a small way a preview of the end of the world. But they were destined to experience still more.

Miles and Miles
6 of Miracles

What heartbreaking scenes of human misery and woe the missionaries saw as they made their way out of Rangoon! It was distressing to see clusters of cars and trucks being burned because no fuel was available and they must not be left to benefit the invading army. Far worse was the sight of hundreds and thousands of weary, hungry, and frightened men, women, and children. The pain caused by the scene was intensified when the men heard that about two hundred weary people had climbed onto the rooftops of an evacuee train and had been swept off to a mangled death when the train went under a low-hanging bridge.

The second day, the four men parted company with evacuees on foot, at the town of Prome. The foot travelers would cross the river and the hills beyond, through Akyab to Chittagong. The men in the cars headed for Maymyo, where the North Burma workers had temporary headquarters.

By eight-thirty that evening they reached Taung-dwingyi, nearly three hundred miles from Rangoon. They were relieved, but also very weary and thirsty, having run out of water several hours earlier. Providentially they found men of a Royal Air Force company staying at the high school, having come to evacuate their women. The missionaries were welcomed to stay there, even though all the men had to sleep on the ground. One of the men went to fill their waterpots, but the water had been shut off at sunset.

Just at the right time a young man recognized Pastor Christensen, having attended tabernacle meetings held by the pastor in Rangoon. The young man was happy to provide water and food. The missionaries praised God for keeping His promise of sure bread and water.

In the morning the missionary men packed their cars and checked their oil and petrol. Eric found he did not have enough fuel to get to Maymyo, two hundred miles away, and would have to try to burn kerosene to stretch fuel for that distance. He gave this bit of information to Mr. Meleen. A truck driver nearby heard him and boomed out, "Gettin' low on petrol, buddy? I think I could let y' have a tin."

Surprised, Eric stammered his thanks as the trucker brought a two-gallon can of gasoline.

As the can emptied into the tank, the benefactor asked, "Do y' think it'll hold another?"

"It sure will," Eric answered gratefully.

"Well, I think I could let y' have another tin." And the second two gallons went in.

This was only typical of a long string of at least minor miracles that kept Eric and his companions going on that long road to safety and freedom. That same day, February 23, the left rear wheel broke on Pastor Christensen's car. That evening the clutch burned out on Mr. Meleen's car. The four travelers began to have serious misgivings as they thought of the road ahead of them. But in each crisis, they found a solution just when it seemed inevitable that the disabled car would have to join the scores of abandoned and burned or burning vehicles they had seen. A bicycle mechanic repaired the burned-out clutch. A friendly oil company executive offered the services of a welder at the site of a big oil rig to weld the broken wheel, and sent the missionaries away with full gasoline tanks and cans, as well.

That day, February 26, as they traveled toward Meiktila, they had to cross ten unbridged rivers. How glad they were that the breakdowns had happened before they reached these perilous crossings.

When they reached Meiktila that evening they found faithful Burmese and Karen press workers still carrying on. The government had taken over the mission school buildings but had allowed the press to continue operating. Eric was especially glad to get the Sabbath school lessons for the coming quarter and a copy of the *Watchman* magazine. And plans were discussed for the press workers to follow if and when the war should reach them.

The next morning the four Rangoon men set out for Maymyo. They were delighted to find there Pastor Wyman, Pastor Baird, and Pastor Skau and his family. To be with friends and to be able to bathe, shave, and wash their clothes seemed a foretaste of heaven. To sleep in a real bed was a most welcome bit of luxury.

Eric and his companions dared to entertain a faint hope of being able to remain in upper Burma. Day by day they followed radio news reports. What little official news came through was given an optimistic slant. Not so with grapevine news. They learned that, led by three thousand liberated convicts, bands of Burmese had looted and plundered the deserted city of Rangoon, carrying away in bullock carts and wagons everything they could lay hands on. Soldiers tried in vain to stop this shameful activity, but even though they shot a band of three hundred ruffians who refused to surrender their plunder, the looting continued until the city was a complete shambles. The missionaries were sick at heart as they thought of the once beautiful city and the homes and belongings they had left behind.

On March 9 the enemy cut the main road at Pegu, and by nightfall Japanese troops entered Rangoon. It was high time to get out of Burma—if possible.

Early the next morning Eric, with Mr. Baird and Mr. Wyman, set off for Mandalay in Baird's Ford Vanette. Mr. Meleen and Mr. Christensen followed in Dr. Walker's car. Mr. Skau and his family expected to fly out a little later. Each car carried thirty gallons of gasoline.

At Mandalay they had been told that they could put both cars on a riverboat and could reach Pakokku, 150 miles down the Irrawaddy River and on the west side, the next morning. This was where a cart track, shown on the map as an irregular dotted line, would be their only possible way left open out of Burma. Their hopes were dashed, however, when they came to the steamship agent and requested passage for themselves and two cars to Pakokku.

"Sorry, gentlemen. There's no hope in the world. All our big passenger ships that can carry cars are more than a week overdue. Evidently someone's got them. We hope it's our own troops and not the enemy."

They learned, however, that one of their cars could be put onto a small ferry to Mingyan, some one hundred miles on the way they wished to go but on the eastern side of the river. Finally, by 10:00 P.M. they finished loading Mr. Meleen's car onto the Mingyan boat. Mr. Meleen and Mr. Christensen were to travel with the car.

An immense crowd of evacuating Indians had hampered their loading, and Eric and the two men with him were now very thirsty and very tired. But they must not linger much longer. A hundred difficult miles lay ahead of them in the Vanette, and they would have to have more fuel. However, their efforts to find any were in vain.

Before daylight the three men in the Vanette left Mandalay. They cheered themselves by recalling God's promises and by recounting evidences of His providential leading in the past. Arriving in Mingyan at noon, they encountered another problem. In the monsoon season the river was six miles wide and came right to the edge of town. Now in the extremely dry season it was about three miles across the river. A bullock driver declared firmly that no car could ever get across.

Leaving Mr. Baird with Dr. Walker's car, Eric and the other men went to see the steamship agent. The agent was sympathetic but held out no hope. The company's small launch could not carry the car, and the large boats were long overdue, their fate unknown. The missionaries almost gave in to discouragement, but again prayer was the answer. They saw the many mat shelters where bullock cart drivers and their beasts rested. They also saw beyond the pontoon wharf forty or more country boats of various sizes unloading their cargo.

Almost simultaneously Eric and Mr. Wyman queried, "Do you suppose we could tie two of those boats together and put some planks across?" Eagerly they hurried off to see, but the boatmen they inquired of refused to consider the idea. At last a tall, rough-looking man heard of the missionaries' proposal and declared he could do the job. After the customary dickering, price and conditions were agreed upon, and an advance payment was made to the boatman. Eric and Mr. Wyman hurried to tell Mr. Baird the good news.

Mr. Baird had good news to tell too. He had made friends with an official who had issued a permit for six gallons of gasoline. After a bite to eat at a rice shop the men proceeded to do what the bullock driver said was impossible. They coaxed the Ford Vanette over the deep sand to the river's edge.

The boatman they had hired had sent a boy to find some planks. At last he came with one plank about twenty feet long, six inches wide, and an inch and a half thick, and two planks about eight feet long, flat on one side and round on the other. Eric couldn't imagine a car riding on planks like those, crosswise on two boats, but the boatman declared he could add bamboo and ropes to strengthen them.

The ferryboat with Mr. Meleen, Mr. Christensen, and Dr. Walker's car on board arrived at the pontoon wharf just at the right time, and the two men were delighted with the prospect of getting both cars farther on the escape route. When Mr. Meleen volunteered the news that the Japanese forces had come thirty-five miles farther north that day above Pegu and had reached Prome on the Irrawaddy, the men decided to transfer the Meleen car from the ferry to the boatman's raft immediately.

Tension and anxiety mounted as coolies lifted and pushed on the car. Mr. Meleen was at the wheel and two guided as they edged the car off the ferryboat onto the planks, until it was at the point of no return. Suddenly there was an ominous cracking sound. Everyone had visions of the car settling to the bottom of the river. Instinctively the coolies pulled back, but Eric shouted for help, and other coolies came to their aid. Almost miraculously the car rolled back onto the little steamer.

The steamer captain agreed to unload the car in the morning. The five missionary men were so exhausted that they lay down to rest on the river's edge. Sleep was impossible. They could hear insolent boatmen boasting loudly what they would do with the cars and luggage if the white men had to abandon them. The men thought about the expanse of the great river and of the enemy advancing hour by hour behind them. Eric literally spent the whole night in prayer.

No answer came until about four o'clock in the morning, when he felt a clear and persistent impression: "Go to the sawmill in the city, the one that was evacuated. Go to the sawmill."

Eric roused the sleeping boatman, saying, "I've been talking to my God all night long, and He has told me to go the sawmill in the city."

The boatman was amazed but agreeable, so they called a bullock cart to take them into town. It was just beginning to get light when they arrived at the huge gates of the sawmill. Surely the place would not be open. But the gates *were* open, and the men went in. They did not see anyone, but they proceeded to select four straight, sturdy planks of suitable dimensions.

Just then they saw a young Burmese lad about 15 years old walking toward them. "Do you wish to buy some timber?" he asked.

"Yes," Eric replied. "When will the clerk come on duty?"

"The clerk will not come today, sir. We closed the mill last week and have evacuated to the other side of the river, but I can sell you the timber. I am the son of the owner. It is strange, sir, but my father woke me about four o'clock this morning and sent me across to get some papers from the office, and I had just come when you drove in."

Eric felt like taking off his shoes, for that dusty lumberyard was holy with the presence of God!

Gratefully and gladly the money was paid and the planks loaded. In silence Eric and the Buddhist boatman walked behind the cart. It was the boatman who broke the reverie. "Your God did help you, didn't He?" he said softly.

By 11:45 A.M. the raft had been finished, the two

cars completely loaded, and they had weighed anchor
and were on their way to Pakokku on the other side of
the river. The men were almost delirious with relief
and gratitude. They bathed, ate, slept, chlorated some
water, and drank their fill. They rejoiced all the day,
and the sun provided a glorious climax as it sank
behind a beautiful bank of golden clouds. All was
peace as they slept that night on an island sandbar.

At 3:00 A.M. the boatman awakened the missionaries. The moon shone brightly, and it would be more
pleasant to travel as far as possible before the heat of
the day. The response was quick and eager. The quiet
beauty of that early morning scene was so glorious
and the wonder of God's deliverance was so moving
that they began to sing:

> " 'All the way my Saviour leads-me;
> What have I to ask beside?
> Can I doubt His tender mercy,
> Who through life has been my guide?
> Heavenly peace, divinest comfort,
> Here by faith in Him to dwell;
> For I know whate'er befall me,
> Jesus doeth all things well;
> For I know whate'er befall me,
> Jesus doeth all things well.' "

Writing of this experience, Eric commented: "Our
voices blended into a harmonious male quartet, and
we sang as we had never sung before. We were singing
part of the Song of Moses and the Lamb, for our
Saviour had made a way for us, a way through the
waters of the old Irrawaddy. We sang till the boatmen
could row no longer but listened spellbound.

"As we sang, I saw the old boatman touch his wife's
hand, and, pointing tremblingly toward us, he whispered, 'They are. They are. Those men are servants of
the living God!' "

As the sun rose the fleeing missionaries could see the gleaming pagodas of Pakokku and the cloudlike smoke of early morning fires. As they drew nearer they saw what looked like a white cloud settled on the riverbank below the city. They were told that this was actually some thirty thousand Indian refugees waiting for boats to take them up the Chindwin River toward the Indian border.

On arrival in Pakokku, the men inquired of the district magistrate about travel conditions on to Tamu. He told them the road was officially closed. Plague and cholera had broken out in the evacuee camps along the way, and many were dying. The road was terrible; only one hundred miles were paved after a fashion, and the other two hundred miles were extremely rough cart tracks.

"But, gentlemen," he said, "cars and busses are getting through in about five days. I think Mr. Sargent and his party went that way about two weeks ago."

Eric and his companions were surprised and happy for this news, for they had understood that the group with Mr. Sargent had taken another route. The kindly demeanor of the magistrate encouraged Mr. Meleen to ask, with startling frankness, "Sir, just what might happen if we chose to proceed without your permission?"

The magistrate paused a moment, then said, "You would have no difficulty with my policemen at this end. Of course, at Tamu they could make you come back, but I hardly think they would." In a lower voice he added, "Gentlemen, if I were in your position I think I would go without delay, but, of course, you understand I cannot give you a permit."

Eric could not believe his ears. The officer who could not give them a permit had advised them to go without delay.

Encouraged by this, Mr. Baird made bold to ask,

"Sir, how many gallons of gasoline do you think we would need for the trip?"

"Busses take eighty gallons," the magistrate carefully replied. "I think a car could get through on forty."

Mr. Baird said, "We have only thirty gallons each. Could you possibly give us a permit to buy a little more?"

"Well, now—under the circumstances, I think—maybe I could," and the magistrate reached for the forms and a pen. "Shall I write, say—twenty-two gallons?"

There was a chorus of fervent thank-you's, and the men went away hardly believing that what they had experienced was real, but preparing to spend a happy and peaceful Sabbath with the small group of believers in Pakokku.

With hearts and fuel tanks overflowing, the missionaries drove slowly out of town to begin the last segment of their long flight to India. The three hundred miles to Tamu took five days. On the way they camped beside still waters, but they also went through the valley of the shadow of death, for they encountered scores of dead and dying, the toll taken by exhaustion, plague, and cholera. It was heart-wrenching to hear the anguished pleas of sick and dying parents begging them to take their children.

At Tamu the men were forced to leave their cars and everything else except the barest necessities. Each was allowed to take sixty pounds, what a coolie would carry with some reluctance, plus thirty to thirty-six pounds each to be carried by the missionaries.

Four painful days were spent crawling up the steep ascents of Tamu Pass, and hobbling down again on the rugged trail. At times they had to endure driving rain; they had very little water and they had meager fare, just a few things that they could cook on the trail.

At last they saw the hills begin to flatten out onto the beautiful plain of Dinapur. There, at the beginning of the India road, busses and trucks picked up evacuees and took them 104 miles to the nearest railway station. All were given free tickets to any place in India to which they wished to go.

Eric and his companions were among twelve hundred evacuees jammed into a train that left Dinapur at 9:00 P.M., March 24. It was a painfully slow but uneventful journey to Calcutta. They arrived there at about 2:00 P.M., March 26. They were first taken to an evacuee camp, where they were able to get a good bath and a good meal. Soon they made contact with church workers and found that Agnes and the children were at Mussoorie. In a few days they were together again, rejoicing and praising God for His providential care.

Eric and his fellow missionaries still held some hope that conditions in Burma would be stabilized somehow so that they might return to the work and the people whom they had learned to love. But each day the news held out less and less reason to hope.

The grim history of World War II tells the story: On April 9, the Japanese bombed Colombo, Cocanada, and Vizagapam, and panic struck India's East Coast. On April 30, Lashio, the Burmese city at the beginning of the Burma Road into China, fell to the enemy. On May 2, Mandalay, the beautiful and proud capitol of Upper Burma, was captured. On May 6, United States forces on Corregidor were compelled to surrender. Later in the month General Stilwell wearily marched out of Burma into India. Eric knew then that his hope to return to Burma was no longer justified.

Late in May the gloom dissipated when word was received from the consul general in Bombay that a ship bound for America would be sailing from Bombay shortly. American evacuees were asked to get ready.

Eric and his family believed that the Lord was opening another way of escape and lost no time in getting ready. Finally the day came to board the troop ship *Brazil.* The twelve hundred passengers spent the next six weeks zigzagging over perilous waters on their way to home, sweet home.

It was strictly wartime travel. Each night portholes were closed tight, light bulbs were removed from each cabin, and much of the night was spent by most of the passengers on the deck. Besides the sixty-nine Seventh-day Adventists on board, there were missionaries from twenty other religious groups. Altogether they totaled 468 individuals. Each night on the blacked-out ship, the hundreds of missionaries sat on the deck and sang. You may be sure Eric helped lead out in that exercise. Two trumpets, two trombones, three violins, a musical saw, and two piano accordions led the singing. Every night the theme song was "Jesus, Saviour, Pilot Me." It was thrilling, and Eric felt that unseen heavenly beings were helping the ship's crew pick their zigzag course through the night and the pathless ocean.

One day a ship ahead of the *Brazil* was sunk by a torpedo. Another ship, one day's travel behind them, met a similar fate. Crews of two ill-fated ships were taken aboard the *Brazil.* These three hundred rescued men were so nervous that they ate and slept with their life belts on.

As they reached mid-Atlantic their ship was met by a Flying Fortress. Passengers and crew gave this friendly military plane a tumultuous welcome as it circled overhead, even for a time after dark. It proved to be a providential escort, for that night a subchaser picked up the vibrations of the *Brazil's* engines and was closing in to investigate when the Flying Fortress dropped a "flaming onion." Just in time the light effectively helped avert a collision disaster.

From the Flying Fortress, information was received that about two days out from their destination the *Brazil* would be met by a destroyer that would escort them until they docked. What a cheering sight to awaken on the designated morning to find the little destroyer right beside the big ship. As it circled around and zigzagged in front of them it communicated information about the course ahead.

Throughout their voyage the passengers had gone through numerous emergency drills. This morning, after being joined by the destroyer, the alarm sounded while many passengers were still eating breakfast. Gun crews rushed to their stations, and all were directed to put on life belts and to assemble on deck.

Eric asked a steward if this was another practice or the real thing, to which the steward replied, "I don't know."

This time passengers really moved! They could see the little destroyer going through strange maneuvers, darting back and forth with all its men in battle array. A signal was given, and three depth charges were dropped overboard, followed by a deafening explosion. The water bubbled and boiled. Then the destroyer fired into the swirling water four shells.

It was hair-raising excitement for the passengers, but they never knew for sure whether this was a real encounter with an enemy submarine or just another practice. In any case it was exciting enough to have been the genuine thing.

One thing was sure—they all knew that by next morning they would be nearly home! That thought brought excitement that exceeded even what they had just been through, for it was the thrill of fulfillment and relief rather than that of uncertainty and danger. Excitement mounted still more when they began to see big red buoys marking a channel to some port.

Eric wrote of this climax to the long and arduous

evacuation story: "We were still yelling and cheering and straining our eyes through the fog for a glimpse of some familiar object that could tell us where we were when suddenly from the forepart of our ship there arose a thunderous roar.

"But nobody said, 'What are they shouting for?' Nobody asked, 'What do you suppose they have seen?' Instinctively everybody knew what it was. There was one mad rush to the port side of the ship, and then we all stood there laughing, crying, shouting, cheering, till we were hoarse; for there, rising from the fog at her feet, with her head and her uplifted arm in the clear morning sunshine, stood 'Old Liberty,' and everybody knew where we were.

"I wish you could have been on that boat that morning to have measured the emotion of those twelve hundred passengers and those three hundred rescued sailor boys when they realized that God had brought them all safely home again.

"Two dear old missionary ladies leaning on the rail just below me were singing 'Praise God, From Whom All Blessings Flow,' and we all joined in, for we all felt just like that. Two others prayed aloud in words, thanking God for bringing us safely home again, and everybody said, 'Amen,' for everybody felt just like that.

"Just then a sailor boy pulled up a chair, mounted it, and, waving his hand affectionately toward 'Old Liberty,' . . . made a speech that I will remember as long as I live. 'Hullo, Mother,' he cried. 'Here are some of your children. Oh, Mother, I'd like to jump right over to you and put my two arms around your neck and give you a big kiss, I would.' And everybody cheered and everybody cried, for everybody felt just like that.

"There stood beside me a sailor boy too overcome with emotion to say a word. For a long time he wiped his eyes and swallowed hard on that horrid lump that was choking the words out of him. Then, thumping me on the elbow, he said, 'Do you know what I'm going to do the very first thing?'

"I said, 'No, my lad, I've no idea what you'll do first.'

" 'Well, do you see that gangplank?'

" 'Yes,' I said, 'what are you going to do with it?'

" 'Well, I'm going off that gangplank, and I'm going to the nearest bit of land I can find, and I'm going to get down on my two knees and I'm going to kiss it, I am, and I don't care who sees me!'

"And truly that's the way you feel when you know your God has brought you out of the fiery iron furnace, across the perilous deep, to home, sweet home, again."

Now let us look briefly at how church members in Burma fared during World War II. When all expatriots had been evacuated, the church members and their national pastors, leaders, and teachers were left on their own resources. Not all that happened in their struggle to survive can be known. Enough is known, however, to reveal their strong faith in a living and powerful God. They literally walked through the valley of the shadow of death, but the Lord was with them and prepared a table before them in the presence of their enemies. They did not escape entirely unscathed, for there were some tragic losses, especially among small children and babies, some of whom could not survive the extreme hardship.

Church members and their leaders were among the thousands who fled from areas targeted by the enemy. Refuge was sought in more remote places, particularly where mission outposts had been established. Leaders who had been trained by the missionaries were towers of strength to their people. They were able to bolster the faith of members when there was not enough food and no medicines at all. God also used them in strange and wonderful ways to witness before officers and guards among the occupying forces.

The long months of war must have seemed endless, and many may have wondered whether the missionaries would ever come back. During the four years of enemy occupation there was no way to get word to or from Burma believers, but members around the world prayed constantly for them, and there was abundant evidence that God had not forgotten or forsaken them.

Two days after Rangoon was retaken by British forces, an Adventist army chaplain who had previously taught at Meiktila Training School flew in with some British troops. As an army chaplain and major he was able to visit church members in several places, gathering information about the fate of many church members and their leaders. He brought welcome news that if all went as planned, Pastor A. J. Sargent would arrive in Rangoon on December 28, 1945, bringing money, food, and clothing. Word was sent out urging all members who could do so to come to the city to share the supplies.

What a meeting it was on New Year's Day, 1946! Pastor Sargent came through without mishap, bringing big boxes of food, clothing, money, and medicines. As they received these gifts the people told of perils, hardships, and suffering as they had fled from their homes to hide in remote jungles. Weeping along with the people, Pastor Sargent told them how in America the church members not only had prayed for the needy and had given general Sabbath school offerings but had contributed and gathered money, food, and clothing to aid fellow believers and others in a land terribly ravaged by war. Now the listeners wept some more, but they were tears of gratitude and joy.

Pastor Sargent surveyed several mission stations,

finding some buildings completely destroyed, others needing major repairs. News that help from abroad was on its way lifted the spirits of the believers. With God's help they felt they could do what needed to be done. Rehabilitation began soon, and by August of 1946 it was possible for officers from the church's Southern Asia Division to visit Burma.

Church workers from all over the Burma Union were called to a central meeting to give reports. Writing of this occasion, Eric Hare reported:

"Amazing as it sounds, although in most places the day schools had been discontinued, Sabbath school and church services were held *every* Sabbath during the occupation. Some of the churches had been bombed. Some had been burned, but that did not stop them. In their temporary huts, in the trenches, or on the mountainsides, they sang their songs of praise and studied the Word of God together *every* Sabbath day, and many souls had been added to the church."

Each worker was given a rehabilitation allowance. One of the first missionaries to come to Burma after the war was Leonard Hare, Eric's son. Leonard and Barnabas Peter had grown up together at Ohn Daw, and now they were put in charge of the mission school, temporarily moved to Myaungmya.

Vivid, thrilling stories, heart-wrenching stories, stories of tragedy and triumph, kept coming from various parts of Burma. In the hysteria of conflict, the very worst traits of fallen human nature were exhibited by the army of occupation. Some church members were arrested and tortured brutally. All Christians were suspected of being spies, and many were treated in a most inhumane manner. Yet in the incidents of extreme cruelty, witnessed for Christ in a strong way. In spite of the rigors they went through, few church members lost their lives.

7 E.B.H.— U.S.A.

Eric and Agnes Hare always believed that among the Karens in Burma had been the "special place" where God wanted them to serve. It was a keen disappointment that war had brought a premature end to their mission service. But now they would carry on, believing that God had called them to another "special place." Twenty years of mission service would strengthen all succeeding ministry.

Apparently the Hares did not find adjustment to the home base difficult. Eric "landed running." They disembarked in New York, July 13, 1942, and they arrived in La Sierra, California, on the 23d. Eric had been asked to serve as secretary of the Sabbath school and radio departments of the Southeastern California Conference. His first official appointment in that field was on August 11, 1942, just nineteen days after their arrival in California. From then on there would be no letup.

On October 1, 1943, Eric was called to be Missionary Volunteer department secretary of the Pacific Union Conference, and the Hares moved to Glendale, California. This move began a strenuous schedule of appearances at churches, schools, evangelistic meetings, workshops, and institutes. His appearances included some at various Protestant churches, civic and social clubs, and radio stations. The word spread that Eric B. Hare had a thrilling story to tell and that he knew how to tell it. A quick tally of his appointments in Arizona and California from August 11, 1942, to May 7, 1946, shows a staggering total of 456 appearances in 211 places. As someone observed, during those years they certainly kept Dr. Rabbit hopping!

Following their harrowing escape from bombed-out Burma, the E. B. Hare family essentially began a new life. Several significant things may be noted:

On September 1, 1942, Eric applied for United States citizenship. That month Peter entered the fourth grade, Verna May the seventh grade, and Leonard began his third year at Pacific Union College in the ministerial course. By this time Eileen, with her husband, Ivan, and their daughter, Ivaleen, were in mission service in Lepi, Angola.

On June 11, 1944, Leonard graduated from PUC. A fortnight later he married Esther Borrowdale in Loma Linda, California, and a few days later the newlyweds left for Washington, D.C., on their way to mission service in India.

The direction Eric's ministry would take is indicated by invitations he received to conduct junior evangelism institutes in three places east of the Rockies during the month of September, 1944. During the next few months, in addition to taking part in junior camps and other activities promoted by his department in his own union conference, he was authorized to lead out in junior evangelism institutes and other training sessions in several places coast to coast.

It is not surprising, then, that on June 22, 1946, Eric was elected to become an associate secretary of the General Conference Sabbath School Department. His love for young people and his proven methods of reaching and teaching junior youth had by now become widely recognized. It was just what the

Sabbath School Department needed, and Eric began at once to put his energy into developing child evangelism through the Sabbath school.

E. B. Hare was in the vanguard of Seventh-day Adventists who recognized the urgent need and almost unlimited potential for specialized soul-winning work among the children and youth of the church and its immediate community. In 1946 only a few voices were being raised in behalf of the children, whose particular needs at the different stages of development were generally not being well met.

Eric's inspirational and instructional book *Those Juniors*, published first in 1946, remains a classic how-to book for teachers and leaders of junior youth. From the perspective of some forty years, it appears that the work of the church in behalf of its children and youth has been revolutionized. Eric B. Hare made a very significant contribution to that phenomenon.

Joining the General Conference departmental staff brought a new dimension to Eric's ministry. The world field was now his "special place," and in the next few years he did have several long overseas itineraries. Workers who followed Eric's footsteps in these world divisions have been made aware of what a tremendous impact his ministry made. At his institutes and workshops, he inspired his hearers with the soul-winning potential of leading and teaching in the Sabbath school. His presentations included *inspiration*, *information*, and perhaps a little *perspiration*, as well. He told hearers *why*, then he told and showed them *how*, and then he coaxed and coached them in the *doing* of it. In those years the Sabbath schools of North America were just beginning to develop the art of illustration, not only through the skill of storytelling in the various children's and youths' divisions but in a special way through the effective use of visual aids.

In Burma the jungle people had little or no formal education, so Eric learned to make teaching very simple, using an everyday vocabulary and visual or verbal illustrations that involved objects, activities, and experiences familiar to his hearers. His "obedience box" stayed at the top of a string held vertically, or slid down, depending upon whether "Johnny" or "Mary" represented by it was obedient. It had a bit of mystery about it that held interest, and it taught lessons that will be recalled by thousands. With an active imagination Eric dreamed up clever offering devices that fascinated children and increased their giving, such as the device in which coins could be seen rolling back and forth down inclines. His paper cutting or tearing and his string manipulation, as well as chemical demonstrations, gained immediate attention and held the interest of his audience.

The Eric B. Hare family arrived in Washington, D.C., on September 5, 1946. It was only a few days later that Eric conducted his first Sabbath school training institute in his new capacity. It was held in Baltimore, Maryland, and was numbered in his notebook as the fifteenth such meeting. It is not clear why he began numbering with fifteen, but one may surmise that he had previously held fourteen institutes outside the conference or union where he held office, and that thus he considered them in the same category as those he would now hold as a General Conference employee.

In any case, from here on, the numbers indicate the extent of his labor and influence and the rigorous schedule he maintained, until his journal entry recorded No. 338, a workshop held in Mount Vernon, Ohio, September 21-23, 1962. His next entry is dated October 1, 1962, and states: "Retired. Went on sustentation and Social Security. But was kept on half time until December, 1963."

Those months after official retirement he spent researching the history of the Sabbath school, and other information on its objectives and activities, data to be used in the forthcoming *Seventh-day Adventist Encyclopedia.* During the same period Eric also was busy writing a junior devotional book for 1965, which was titled *Make God First.*

Numbered items, places, and dates cannot reflect anything of the eagerness and excitement Sabbath school workers felt and expressed as in Eric's workshops they grasped practical principles of learning and simple but effective methods by which to meet the emotional and spiritual needs of children and youth at their different levels of development. They went away from such training sessions fortified to meet the challenge.

Intermingled with Eric's carefully kept items of information are glimpses of personal triumphs and tragedies. We shall note a few of these, for there are bright threads and there are dark threads that make up the warp and woof of life.

The older daughter of Eric and Agnes, Eileen Higgins, and her husband, Ivan, arrived in San Francisco February 27, 1947, on furlough from India. Eric met them in that city and had a half hour to spend with them before leaving for Portland, Oregon, for his next appointment. A few weeks later Eric wrote a letter to friends and fellow workers, a letter full of pathos and pain:

"April 24, 1947

"Get ready for some bad news. Eileen was killed in an automobile accident near Van Horn, Texas, yesterday, April 23, at 2:30 P.M.

"They had arrived in San Francisco on furlough from India, February 27. I had the pleasure of meeting the boat with Ivan's father and mother. Mr. Higgins senior had succeeded in securing a new car, and everybody was so happy, and they had such a lovely time visiting friends in California on their way to Mesquite, New Mexico, where Ivan's folks live. Then after a few weeks' rest they took another trip to the Northwest, visiting friends and relatives at Salt Lake City and in Washington State.

"Their visit to the West completed, they packed up and planned to come to us in Washington, D.C., where Ivan was to work on his Master's degree in the Seminary. They left Mesquite in the morning, and Ivan drove about 140 miles to Van Horn on Highway 80. Here Eileen suggested that she take the wheel while Ivan had a rest. Ivan put his head down and dozed off. The next thing he knew the car was swaying. He started up, saw they were on the wrong side of the road. There was no traffic. The car swayed to the right, then to the left, and then everything blacked out. The car turned over; Eileen was thrown out; all were knocked unconscious. When Ivan came to, a car that had been about a mile away drew up and gave assistance. Ivan had bruises on the head and body. So did the little girls, but none was serious. But Eileen had a bad bruise over the right eye, another on the back of the neck, and a broken collarbone. They were only fifteen miles out of Van Horn, but she never regained consciousness and died on the way to the hospital. She died about half way home from San Francisco. I suppose we will never know what caused the accident.

"Poor Agnes never saw her. She heard her over the telephone from San Francisco for a few minutes, and she will hear that happy voice no more. Only a few days before, Eileen wrote to Grandma Fulton, who had been very close to death with influenza, and said, 'You just mustn't die, Grandma. We'll soon be there and we must see you.' Grandma didn't die, but Eileen did, and she won't see Grandma after all. Poor Grandma! It was just two years to the very day and almost the very hour that Grandma Fulton had passed away, and she wept as she said, 'Why couldn't it have been me?'

"Just that morning at breakfast we had been talking of their coming, and we had a little game of prophesying the date of their arrival. I thought it would be May 6. Mother said May 5; Peter said May 4; and Verna May said she thought they would arrive on her birthday, May 2. We were so happy over it and so excited. Mother said she could hardly wait. Eileen will come, all right, but she will come in a coffin. The little granddaughters will come too, but they will be motherless little orphans.

"We are planning the funeral here in Washington, D.C., and we cannot begin to tell you how stunned and crushed our hearts are. But as Paul expressed it, so we feel—'We are troubled on every side, yet not distressed; we are perplexed, but not in despair; persecuted, but not forsaken; cast down, but not destroyed.'

"Drinking deeply of the cup of sorrow,
                    "We are yours truly."

On a happier note, Verna May graduated from the academy in Takoma Park, Maryland, May 24, 1947. Having learned to read lips in the special Oakland school, she was now able to attend a regular school. She did have to request one teacher to shave off his mustache so that she could see his lips! At the same time Peter finished the eighth grade. As months went by, Ivan Higgins found a new wife and his children a new mother when he married Phyllis Borrowdale on October 30, 1947. On February 26 the next year they left San Francisco, bound for mission service in Rangoon, Burma.

Perhaps the greater tragedy, because the situation caused Eric and Agnes to alternate between hope and despair for so many years, was the health and related problems from which Verna May suffered progressively. The effects of her childhood illness became more and more pronounced as the years went by.

Verna May met a young man who also had become deaf from a childhood illness, and they were married in 1950 in Takoma Park, Maryland. They moved to Oregon, where two children, Steven and Debbie, were born, both with normal hearing. Unfortunately, it was not long before Verna May had to be hospitalized and was unable to carry on as a wife and mother. She underwent several surgeries and was in and out of hospitals. In a letter dated May 21, 1976, Eric describes the close of Verna May's life of frustration and suffering:

"You will be sad to hear that Verna May passed away May 16, 1976. Yet you will feel relief in knowing that since she had suffered a great deal, she is now at rest.

"You are more or less familiar with her deafness and the frustrations of her younger life. . . . In 1973 and in 1974 she had surgery for cataracts. In August, 1975, a malignancy was found in one of her breasts, and she had a mastectomy operation. Three months later they discovered she had cancer in her back, her legs, her liver, and her lungs, and a tumor on her brain.

"She was greatly loved by the doctors and nurses, and they did everything possible to check the malignancies. The X-rays and chemotherapy helped a little, but in three months it was apparent that her condition was hopeless. . . .

"Most of the days she was in a semicoma, but in between she had bright days when she could understand and ask questions. Debbie cabled when her little daughter, Ilse, was born. Verna May smiled and seemed to understand that she was now a grandmother.

"Then on May 16, about 7:00 A.M., she passed away. Father and Mother Hare and Peter drove to Michigan from Takoma Park, Maryland, and with Leonard and his wife, Esther, and our dear friend Mrs. Kirby, we laid her to rest.

For some time Eric and Agnes had cared for Verna May's children, Steven and Debbie, when they were young. Eric had taught both of them to play the trumpet, and he was proud of Debbie's ability on the piano. With Peter and Steven he played trumpet trios on several occasions before Steven went away to academy.

Insights into Eric's unique personality can be received by reading letters he wrote and rather whimsical accounts of outstanding emotional experiences. For example, almost a year before Verna May's death, Eric and Agnes celebrated their sixtieth wedding anniversary. They did not want a public celebration, but on that occasion Eric described their joy in a write-up for the family, "Guess What Happened to Us":

"June 24 was our sixtieth wedding anniversary. We didn't want any fuss made over it. We decided just to sneak off by ourselves and have a Chinese dinner. But, lo, and behold, four days before the eventful day an official-looking envelope came in the mail. It contained a card from Gerald Ford, the President of the United States! He and the first lady were congratulating us for attaining our sixtieth, diamond, anniversary. Who told him? We wonder *who done it.*

"We thought we would supply flowers for Sabbath school that weekend, so we contacted the lady in charge. When we got to Sabbath school, lo and behold, there were the flowers. They were beautiful, all right, but there was also a paragraph in the church bulletin, stating that the flowers were provided by Elder and Mrs. Eric B. Hare on the occasion of their sixtieth wedding anniversary. Then began the handshakes, the back pats, and congratulations. The pastor called us to the platform at the beginning of the church service and said a lot of nice things, and the people said Amen! You know what? We don't need to die. All the nice things have already been said. But who told him? We wonder *who done it.*

"Well, the big day came, June 24. Agnes and I exchanged our personal cards at the break of dawn and made our plans for a quiet little Chinese dinner (which is a Hare ritual), but ere we sat down for morning worship there was a knock at the door, and in came Eric and May Howse with a card and a wedding cake! We had hardly said Amen to our morning prayer when the telephone rang. It was Peter and Patti wishing us the best. After clearing away the dishes we had a little shopping to do, and when we got back the postman had been there, and there were letters and cards all over the front-room floor. Cards and best wishes from fellow workers, relatives, friends, and used-to-be junior campers. A knock on the door, a telephone call, a knock, a call, and so it went till 1:00 P.M., when we sneaked out to go to the Shanghai Chinese Restaurant in Silver Spring. Who could have told all of these people? We wonder *who done it.*

"In the confusion of the heavy traffic in Silver Spring, I went through a red light. In two seconds I could see a cop was on my tail. So I pulled over and waited for him. He asked me the usual questions, and when he hesitated a moment, I said, 'I'd be glad if you didn't have to give me a ticket today, for this is our sixtieth wedding anniversary.'

"'Your sixtieth wedding anniversary?' he gasped, and then said, 'Congratulations!' and waved us on.

"The dinner was great, and for dessert we drove by the Dairy Queen and had a frozen custard cone (also a

Hare ritual). Do you know, that cop was the nicest cop we ever met, and we began to feel we didn't care *who done it.*

"When we got home there were more cards all over the floor (from the letter slot in the door). We were still reading them when two brethren from the GC Public Relations Department came. For two hours they took pictures and asked us how it felt to be married sixty years. And that's one thing we knew, and we told them. They had hardly gone when there was a long-distance call. It was from Verna May. From Verna May! Bless her. It was a great day and will long be remembered. We have our suspicions, we've got a pretty good idea who told everybody our secret. But actually we don't care now *who done it.*

"God bless them and give them a happy sixtieth Wedding Anniversary."

It seems that with the passing of Verna May, for whom Eric and Agnes had such deep sympathy, Eric's zest for an active and exciting life began to diminish. The toll of years was laying its heavy hand on him. Frailties to which mankind is heir made themselves felt. He had had cataracts removed from both eyes, and his peripheral vision was defective.

November 8, 1976, Eric had a fender-bender accident with his car. Just when he was wondering what to do, a man appeared, seemingly out of nowhere, and said, "Elder Hare, I know that you don't know me, but I was one of your junior-camp boys thirty years ago." It was Jim Davis, an employee in the General Conference Insurance Service. He took care of all the details of the emergency.

Eric thought about the accident for a couple of days and decided his eye condition would no longer permit him to drive, so without turning back he gave up driving. Of course, this significant milestone prompted another write-up, which he concluded with these words:

"For several days after that, my friend Jim guided me through the red tape till all was well again.

"But how come a little boy remembered for thirty years and turned up just when he was needed so much?

"I've heard some people say that when a good man dies he turns into an angel. But I know some good people who turn into angels while they are still alive—ANGELS UNAWARES."

Reluctantly Eric had to say No when asked to tell stories at Vacation Bible School or Sabbath school. And he could no longer conduct the Week of Prayer for the younger children at the John Nevins Andrews School, as he had for many years. This inability was felt keenly. But he still had the joy of knowing that his life had not been lived in vain. He recorded this joy for the family:

IT MUST BE I'M GOING TO DIE

"You know how at a funeral everybody remembers the nice things the dead person has done? Well, that is what has happened to me. People go out of their way to tell me how their children and their children's children have enjoyed my stories and have literally worn out my books reading them over and over again.

"One dear brother said, 'I can never forget the Sabbath school workshop you held in Nigeria twenty years ago, the object lessons, the stories, the songs!' and he burst into singing:

"'I will wear a crown
In my Father's house.
There'll be JOY! JOY! JOY!'

"Now, how come he remembered twenty years and took the trouble to tell me? It's not natural to do that. It must be I'm going to die, and that's why!

"You know how when church is dismissed there is a bit of a traffic jam near the front door? Well, the other day I was inching my way through the crowd going out of church when I felt a little love-poke on my hand. I looked down quickly and saw a little 6-year-old squashed up between the grownups. When she saw I noticed her, her face broke into the sweetest smile, and her little hand waved the sweetest hello. You know I'm nearly blind, but I was so glad I could still see enough to catch the love in that smile. I could not recognize her, but she remembered me, and what a lift it gave me!

"How come little folks do things like that, that make me so happy? It must be I'm going to die and that's why."

Eric and Agnes continued living in their home and managed very well. They enjoyed playing a game of Scrabble at four o'clock every afternoon until Eric's eyesight failed. But then it became more and more difficult to care for their home. In the following soliloquy, Eric exhibited his Christian philosophy, looking in faith for the fulfillment of God's promises:

OH, HORRORS!

"The other day I turned 84.
Friends have taken time to pause and say, 'Many happy returns, old man.'
And the mantle shelf is decked with cards
that also say, 'Many happy returns.'
But I say, 'Oh, horrors!'

"During 1978 not only have the years increased in number—
My hair is whiter,
My shoulders are stiffer, and
My left eye is dimmer.
'Oh, horrors!'

"It's harder to shave,
 It's harder to eat,
 It's harder to bathe,
 It's harder to dry.
 'Oh, horrors!'

"Agnes has to make my food bite-size,
 Agnes has to comb my hair,
 Agnes has to dry me after I bathe,
 Agnes has to give me her arm when we walk,
 Agnes has to read all our letters,
 Agnes has to answer them all, too.
 'Oh, horrors!'

"Who said, 'Many happy returns'?
 Just wait till you're past 80,
 Wait till you're past threescore and ten,
 Wait till your 'get up and go' has got up and went;
 Then you will know why I say,
 'Oh, horrors!'

"But there are some things that have truly been
 happier,
 Some things that have brightened the way.
 They are the true and precious promises recorded
 in God's Word.
 Then let the horrors come,
 Let them do their worst.
 They will soon be banished completely,
 and then we will have our 'happy returns' forever
 and ever more."

A Short Man Casts
8 a Long Shadow

At five feet nine inches tall, Eric B. Hare was not excessively short, but the point is that for a modest and unassuming person, he cast an exceptionally long shadow of influence that has been far-reaching and long-lasting.

We have already chronicled Eric's dedication to his task, his willingness to accept assignments and appointments. During his full-employment years he seemed to brush aside concern for his own well-being and comfort. Equally impressive, or more so, is the record of his activities after retirement.

Eric kept careful records of his postretirement appointments: sermons, Sabbath school mission talks, stories in various Sabbath school divisions, devotional and inspirational talks and stories in youth meetings and at junior camps, inspirational presentations at workshops, trumpet solos and participation in instrumental duets and trios, stories and demonstrations at Vacation Bible Schools, and perhaps more! All these occupied many retirement days.

Eric was officially retired on October 1, 1962. His first recorded appointment thereafter was on February 2, 1963, His last entry was for an appointment on April 24, 1976.

He met a total of 419 appointments in 48 different places, most of them in the Washington, D.C., area, but some notable ones as far away as California. The tally is even more impressive when it is noted that in most instances Eric would make presentations to three or more groups in one day in the same location. Records show that from 1963 through 1976 Eric made at least 782 presentations. And that was called retirement!

Eric's sermons were rich with practical, down-to-earth, easy-to-understand-and-remember illustrations. His stock of stories seemed endless and he used them with consummate skill. No doubt this is why he is remembered more especially as a peerless storyteller and writer than in any other role. Just where and how Eric learned the art of storytelling is not known. He possessed an analytical and imaginative mind. His exposure to the Karen culture in Burma may have been a stimulus, for the Karens have a great stock of stories that are often told.

An interesting insight into the matter of Eric's storytelling is afforded by a letter written to him by Arthur W. Spalding, himself an accomplished story-teller and writer, author of the book *Christian Storytelling.* Spalding wrote in part:

"You are the topmost storyteller in the denomination, and God and yourself made it such. I appreciate your modesty and the praise you give me, which is far beyond my desserts. I believe you believed what you once told me, that you could not tell stories until you found my book; but I don't believe it. . . . I am no such prestidigitator as to be able to pull a Hare out of a silk-hatted book on storytelling. You had the genius; possibly I helped you polish it a little. But I never had your talent in storytelling or in 'enthusing' other people to tell stories. You are a genius, good friend."

A stroll through the Eric B. Hare memorabilia yields fascinating insights into his personal value system. Pictures, invitations to notable affairs, certificates of completion or achievements, citations (including one for exceeding the posted speed limits in a California town), copies of publicity items, program folders of all kinds, especially from band concerts. A band concert was one type of performance Eric simply could not resist. When he was in town he always attended concerts by the United States service bands, held on the Capitol steps or in a band shell on the Potomac River at Watergate. Band music seemed to stir his soul and to give him a positive outlook on life.

A generous collection of resource materials provides insights into Eric's philosophy of life. Examples are these: the poem "Don't Quit," the short essay "Keep at Your Work," and a whimsical squib that had been reprinted from the *Tex-Ark Times.* It reads:

"New York *Journal-American* columnist Doug Welch reported on the 'finest business letter' story related to him by a prominent business consultant. The letter, obviously written by an illiterate salesman:

" 'Dear Boss: I seen this outfit which they ain't never bought a dime's worth of nuthin from us and sole them a couple hundred thousand dollar's worth of guds. I am now goin to Chawgo.'

"Two days later a second letter arrived at the home office:

" 'I cum hear an I sole them half a milyon,' it said.

"Both letters were posted on the bulletin board with a note appended by the company president:

" 'We been spendin too much time tryin to spel, insted of tryin to sel. Let's watch them sails. I want everboddy should reed these letters from Gooch who is on the rode doin a grate job for us, and you should go out and do like he done.' "

Eric was always delighted with the notes and letters of appreciation he received. His files are full of them, at least 165 of them, coming from thirty States and from twelve countries outside of North America. There was an exceptional response to the serialized story of Dr. Rabbit, as well as to the same story in book form.

"Thank you" and "We love you and your stories" messages were written to him by children and youth from 7 to 18 years of age. Some children as young as 5 persuaded adults to write in their behalf. Adults also wrote for themselves. Some were grandmothers or even great-grandmothers, from 67 to 90 years of age. The Dr. Rabbit series emphasized the "special place" concept that Eric's mother taught him to believe in and to prepare for. The responses reflect the positive impact of this concept.

Try to picture what this outpouring of appreciation and affection must have meant to this man already seven years into retirement. He could look back with real satisfaction to those pioneer mission years and the miracles of transformation in the lives of the Karen jungle people. He could recall with humble gratitude the series of miracles that enabled him and his family to escape the perils and horrors of a bloody war. Now to realize that the telling of those adventures with God would be a witness to which young and old would respond with a commitment to find and occupy that "special place" God had for them—this must have brought a marvelous sense of fulfillment.

Here is a letter of appreciation that is a good wrap-up of juvenile sentiments and interests, but written in an astonishingly mature style:

"Dear Dr. Rabbit:

"I enjoyed your series of stories so much! I have read your books—*The Haunted Pagoda, Clever Queen, Jungle Stories,* and *Jungle Storyteller*—and enjoyed every one of them!

"When I was small, my older brother and I wore out

two record player sets from playing Dr. Rabbit's phonograph records so much! I still remember those stories: 'Bunny and Jim,' 'The Big Yellow Truck,' 'Mister Crooked Ears,' 'The Hermit and the King,' and well—I could still think of more titles!

"I also remember camp meeting at Gladstone Park of the Oregon Conference several years ago. You came to the Kindergarten pavillion and told the story of Me Me. You may not remember it. But I do. Because I was one of the little girls sitting there with big wide eyes listening intently to every word of your story. . . .

"I especially like what you said in the last chapter of your story in the *Guide*. 'God has a special place for you. When you find that place you'll know it, and you'll have the truest happiness in this life, right here.'

"And do you know something? I am praying that God will guide me into my special place of service.

"You asked in your last chapter, 'What are you going to do when you grow up?'

"Well, may I say right here that I want to do what God wants me to do.

"God has given us guidelines by which we can realize just what we should do for the finishing of His work. Those guidelines are impressions and talents from Him.

"I love to write and write stacks of papers—stories, poems, and articles.

"Can you guess what I want to be and what I think God wants me to be?

"Well, it's my ambition to become the editor of one of our church papers. And even though I'm only 12 and in the seventh grade, God can guide my life. I can see His guidelines.

"Say, but I'm glad God leads! Dr. Rabbit, aren't you?

"Yours in God's leading,
"Jean

"P.S. My grandmother told me to tell you that she enjoyed Dr. Rabbit's stories too!"

Among these thank-you letters is one written by one who has herself become known for her well-written and interesting stories and as editor of the denomination's children's periodical *Guide*. These are her words:

"Dear Dr. Rabbit:

"As a child I read and reread *Clever Queen*, fascinated by the beliefs of the jungle people. I talked about the fry smell, one's kalar, and the superiority of the rabbit. To this day I can repeat the song that Clever Queen's new mother sang to her. To my surprise, I was even more enchanted by the Dr. Rabbit series. Please, please put it into book form. I want it for my little girl to have in her library.

"Thank you for your inspiring story and the delightful manner in which it was told.

"Sincerely,
"Penny Wheeler (Mrs. Gerald Wheeler)"

These have been a very small sampling of the flood of messages of appreciation for Elder Hare's stories. Significantly, the majority of the writers of the messages included a pledge to pray for divine guidance in seeking and finding the "special place" of service God had for them. It would seem that a man who had carried heavy burdens for many years and who was seven years into his official retirement would have been overwhelmed by the volume of messages received, yet Eric answered every letter, note, and card personally. Such was the dedication of one who had committed himself to guide young people especially to make it their goal in life to fit into God's great and loving purposes for their lives.

The Trumpeter and
9 the Trumpet

Eric Hare, God's man, surely philosophized that "it is better to wear out than to rust out"! He accepted scores of appointments after his book *Dr. Rabbit* came off the press and prompted a shower of thank-you messages. There were junior and youth camps, camp meetings, camps for blind youth, elementary school Weeks of Prayer, Vacation Bible Schools, trumpet trios with his son and grandson, and much more. During the period 1971-1973, Eric also prepared three sets of Bible lessons for the General Conference Department of Education.

Eric's lifework, and certainly his retirement career, reached its zenith, at least in emotional impact, in 1969, when he and Agnes made an extended trip in their 1967-model Rambler. They left Takoma Park on June 12, bound for the West Coast, making ten stops on the way to visit friends and relatives. He left Agnes at her sister Jessie's home and arrived at the Central California Conference youth camp in Yosemite National Park, July 1.

Eric had been invited by Winston DeHaven, conference youth director, to assist in camp activities as a special featured guest at the season's first junior camps. It was an experience long remembered by campers and staff alike. The following letter from the camp director summarizes the response to Elder Hare's camp ministry:

"Dear Dr. Rabbit:

"There are not enough words in the English language, or the Burmese language, for that matter, to express our deep gratitude to you for spending three happy and memorable weeks at Camp Wawona.

"The staff and campers all grew very close to you, as you know. It was amazing to me how the Lord blessed you in strength for the many tasks we asked you to do. The Camp Council period, the continued story, the mission stories, the Sabbath worship hours, and playing the trumpet for flag raising and lowering were more than we could have expected. In addition, each of us wants to thank you once more for the "Magic Box" that was given with love. It is something each of us will treasure and be able to use as we talk with boys and girls. . . .

"You know, of course, that each of us loves and appreciates you far more than we can say. To say Thank you seems so inadequate, but from the bottom of our hearts we do say a most sincere and heartfelt thanks to you for making these three weeks at Camp Wawona days to always be remembered. We shall look forward to a great reunion with you and your lovely wife and all your many other friends from around the world when He comes again, but we are a bit selfish in requesting just one thing—please let us have our own private Camp Wawona reunion with you. To this event we are all looking forward. . . .

"May God bless you always."

    "Always your friend,
    Winston C. DeHaven
    Youth Director"

Characteristically, Eric wrote out the following comments concerning his feelings and responses to the Camp Wawona experience:

You may remember that thirty-five years ago [1934], while I was MV secretary for Northern California, it was my pleasure to take the juniors from Northern California in to the Wawona Junior Camp in Yosemite. I went twice a year, once with the boys and once with the girls. My last visit to Wawona was twenty-four years ago, when I went in as Pacific Union MV secretary. Well, it appears that my old junior campers are now the fathers and mothers of this present generation of juniors, and they began to beg Elder W. C. DeHaven, Central California MV secretary, to ask me to come to Wawona just once more and tell *their* children some stories before I passed away. So when Elder DeHaven wrote me an urgent invitation last Christmas time, I agreed to attend two junior camps this summer, July 6-20.

"Accordingly Agnes and I got all packed up and left Takoma Park in my little Rambler, June 12. We stayed for the weekend with Lenny at Berrien Springs, and attended the wedding of [our granddaughter] Penny and Ken Thachuck, June 15. By June 20 we were at St. Helena, where we visited for a week with friends and relatives. Then we spent the weekend of June 27-29 in Oakland. June 30 we drove to Pearblossom, where Agnes' sister, Jessie, lives. Agnes stayed with Jessie while I was at junior camps, and had a nice visit with [granddaughters] Maureen and Ivaleen and others around Loma Linda.

"I drove in to Wawona on July 3 to avoid the July 4 rush, and could not believe I was at junior camp. In my day we pitched tents, lived very primitively, and swam in the icy-cold river. But now modern cabins with hot-and-cold showers and inside toilets, to house seven campers and a counselor, took the place of the tents, and the original camp circle could look after up to one hundred girls. Up the hill a little, another section of cabins, a tepee camp, and a wagon camp could look after one hundred boys! I shared a cabin with another worker. It had a hot-and-cold shower and a toilet. Fancy having hot water to shave with at junior camp! It just didn't seem right. And to make it more unbelievable, there was a large, modern heated swimming pool!

"Well, Brother DeHaven wasn't too sure what this *old* man could do, and I must confess I was not too sure what I could deliver either. But the Lord surely blessed us, and when 126 second-generation juniors came in for the first camp and all shiny-eyed said, "My mother used to be one of your junior campers,' 'My father was too,' 'My grandma was one of your assistants,' et cetera, et cetera, all fear and timidity vanished, and the old fire came back and I let them have it. Character talks with magic object lessons were at nine o'clock every morning, and "Haunted Pagoda" continued every night at campfire. Now, it just happened that that same week the *Guide* began publishing my series of eight Dr. Rabbit stories. So in no time I was Dr. Rabbit, and enthusiasm was running high.

"At the end of the first camp, they made nine speeches and presented me with two camp shirts, making me an official member of the staff. Twenty of the juniors asked their parents if they could stay for the second camp, too. So I had to reload and give another set of talks, and told 'Clever Queen' for campfire. We had 178 at the second camp, 11 to 16 years old. By this time the regular bugler had gone to Switzerland for the youth congress there, so I became the bugler for reveille, the flag, and taps. At the close of the second camp they named the biggest sugar pine tree (three feet in diameter) at the campfire circle the Eric B. Hare Tree, and put my name on it with a brass plate!

"Then Brother DeHaven begged, "Please, Dr. Rabbit, stay for one more camp; we can't get along without you now." So I rang up Agnes and she said

OK. So I stayed for the third camp. By this time we all knew one another, and it was real fun.

" 'There are only about one hundred signed up for the third camp,' said Brother DeHaven. But twenty from camp two stayed over, and forty new ones came, so we had 160!

"Well, at the end of the third camp I told my last story and had just said Goodbye and blown them some kisses when two of the men caught me by the arms and said, 'Brother Hare, you come with us.' They marched over to an easy chair and sat me down. Two girls came up with a banner, reading, 'Dr. Rabbit, we love you,' and held it over me, and two of the nature teachers, Jim Chase and his wife, put on a panto-mime-type 'This Is Your Life' program. As they read the story, the different ones enacted different scenes in our life, mostly from *Irish Boy and God*. They had me learning to pray at my mother's knee. Going to college. Picking figs for Agnes and saying, 'I love *you!*' They showed me in Burma becoming Dr. Rabbit and ended up with Dr. Rabbit coming to Wawona Junior Camp. By this time my chin was crinkling and I was gulping, but they were not finished yet.

"Brother DeHaven made a final speech and pre-sented me with an engraved bronze plaque expressing their appreciation, and two hundred campers stood and clapped and cheered for I don't know how long. Then they wanted a speech from me, and all I could say was 'I feel as if I have been loved to death, but it is an awfully nice way to die.' Then I blew them some more kisses. It was an hour or more before the snapshots and handshaking were finished. Then I played taps and went to bed and cried myself to sleep.

"Next morning I slipped out of camp before anyone was up. I found Agnes had had all the visiting she wanted for one holiday, so we started off back home the next morning."

Elder Hare made many more public appearances following the Wawona Junior Camp, but it appears that that experience was quite a climactic one. Obviously he was greatly pleased with the special citation given him there. This is the way the final paragraph reads:

> "WHEREAS—we want to make this an historic occasion for us and for you, as well as for all who attend Camp Wawona in the future "WE DO HEREBY—with great PRIDE, HONOR AND DIGNITY—dedicate the tall, majestic sugar pine bordering the back of our campfire bowl, to you, our dear friend, and it will be known and remembered from this day on as the ERIC B. HARE TREE."

A tall, straight, majestic tree, with roots thrust deep into the solid earth, its trunk reaching upward as it grows toward the blue heavens—a fitting symbol of the kind of person Eric B. Hare was: down-to-earth, deeply rooted in solid convictions concerning the love of God, received and shared; in personal devotional life constantly reaching up for guidance and blessing from above.

The trip to Wawona was the last long journey Eric and Agnes took. Numerous invitations after that took him no farther than Kalamazoo, Michigan. This was a great change of pace for one who had traveled so extensively. His carefully kept records indicate that from 1915 through 1974 he had preached 15,115 sermons and was involved in 3,529 other meetings. During that time span he recorded the following distances, according to mode of travel:

By car...249,752 mi.   By ship or launch...218,612 mi.

By bus... 24,066 mi.   By plane...171,084 mi.

By train...310,692 mi. Total Mileage...974,206 mi.

Eric's records were not to draw admiration or praise. Never did he make a public parade of these details or in any way call attention to his accomplishments. Rather, it must have been a source of comfort and satisfaction to him to be able to look back to see what the Lord could do with one person wholly dedicated to the will and work of God in his "special place." Like the apostle Paul, Eric could say, "I have fought a good fight, I have finished my course, I have kept the faith."

The poignancy of those years of cutting loose from a very active and meaningful life comes through in a little reverie in which Eric wrote out some of his emotions. He gave it the title "Bye-bye, Crooked Ears."

"Old age has its sad days.
Like the day I had to give up driving my car.
And the day I stopped playing my trumpet.
And the day I had to stop telling stories.
And the day I had to say No to a request to help in a Vacation Bible School.
Yes, it's sad. Sad, sad!
Well, a few years ago I helped with my last Sabbath school workshop.
I often looked longingly at my big suitcase in which I used to to carry around my object lessons and story illustrations.
But I simply couldn't part with them—not yet!
There was the picture of Limpy, the little monkey that saved the life of a little 1-year-old baby boy.
There was the little box that slid up and down on a string and stopped when I wanted it to.
There was the converted heathen that looked

like Jesus when I took his devil charms off.

There was Me-Me, the Chinese Lady, and Crooked Ears!

What could I do with them? What could I do *for* them?

To do nothing would be like burying them alive.

I couldn't do that to my Sabbath school children.

No! No! I must give them away. Yes, give them away!

So I chose a good Sabbath school lady and carefully, lovingly explained them to her and gave them to her.

She was delighted, and promised to be good to them.

I watched her go to her car and put her new treasures on board.

And I—I brushed a tear from my eyes and whispered,

'Bye-bye, Limpy; bye-bye, Me-Me; bye-bye, Crooked Ears.

Bye-bye. I may never see you again, but I'll never forget you.

Bye-bye.' "

It is interesting to discover a rather unusual continuity of activity running through the greater part of Eric's life. You will recall his lifelong love affair with brass bands in general and with the trumpet in particular. Philosopher Chu Ching, who lived in the sixth century B.C., observed that "for changing people's manners and altering their customs, there is nothing better than music." During his mission career in Burma, Eric proved the truth of that statement. When he and his fellow workers at the Ohn Daw Mission Station had tried in vain to coax people to come to the station for help offered there, it was Eric's cornet, you will recall, that drew villagers like a magnet.

When the Eric Hare family returned to the United States permanently, the trusty trumpet was still a real assset. In his later years, in the Washington, D.C., area, with his son Peter and grandson Calvin, Eric performed in trumpet trios that were always greatly appreciated. This three-generation trio gave their last performance on October 14, 1978, a short time after Eric's seventy-ninth birthday.

Just a year before his death it became apparent that Eric and Agnes could no longer be independent. It was arranged for them to move into an apartment in the home of their son Leonard, in Berrien Springs, Michigan. For a time, with minimal help they were able to care for themselves, surrounded with familiar treasures.

A combination of physical problems caused Eric's condition to worsen so that late in May it was necessary to move him to the Berrien Springs General Hospital. On June 1 when the family came to visit, there was no response from him. At six-thirty that evening someone from the hospital called to say that the end had come peacefully for Elder Hare.

For a clear description of the close of Eric's earthly career, let us quote from a letter written to family members and close friends by Leonard and Esther Hare;

"In keeping with Dad's wishes, the funeral and burial took place in the D.C. area. Peter and Patti arranged the visitation and the funeral services and got out the word. Many dear old friends and battle-scarred warriors came to honor and pay tribute to our dad. It seems the only things people remembered were happy, joyous events. Often it was more a celebration than the weeping and mourning one has come to associate with funerals.

"Dad would have approved the service. His associates who were young when he was in his prime gave him a farewell that would have honored a king. Elder Bill Murrill read the eulogy. Elder Curtis Barger, a Sabbath school colleague, presented the biographical sketch. In this he was helped by Dad himself, who had recorded dates and events in the meticulously kept *Hare Book.* Elder Melvin Adams honored Dad with a spirited trumpet rendition of 'When the Roll Is Called Up Yonder.' It was exactly the right touch! Elder John Hancock, who worked with Dad in junior camps in the early days in California, preached the sermon. He touched on Dad's skills as a storyteller and communicator. He punctuated his sermon effectively with 'Don't you know? Haven't you heard? Hasn't anybody ever told you?' Elder Eugene Crane, who followed Dad at Ohn Daw, offered the closing prayer. Recorded band music was played during the recessional. Dad couldn't have planned it better himself!

"The Karen community in the Washington area turned out to bid farewell to Thara Pa Doh ("Big Teacher") or Pu Po Deh ("Grandfather Rabbit"), as they fondly called him. Dad's links with the Karens of Burma have always been something special. No Sabbath afternoon worship with Lenny and Esther was complete without singing hymns and repeating the Lord's Prayer in Karen. Once during his final month, his mind strayed a little. Lenny found him dressed in his pajamas, two suitcases and his beloved trumpet . . . on his bed, and he was busily packing. 'Where are you going, Dad?' Lenny asked. 'Your mother and I are going back to Ohn Daw,' Dad replied.

"Many of the nurses and aides at the Berrien General Hospital had grown up on Dad's stories. When they knew their patient was *the* Dr. Rabbit they formed a circle of love and care around Father that astonished the doctor. 'Money could never buy the care he is getting,' he exclaimed to Lenny."

This spontaneous outpouring of love and appreciation on the part of the Dr. Rabbit Patrol was a touching tribute to one whose life of deeply caring ministry had reached out to bless so many other lives. Their concern and care was constant, around the clock, during Eric's last days and hours. Thus, in the words of the psalmist, God "giveth his beloved sleep."

Thus the life story of the beloved storyteller is ended— No! Not really ended, but interrupted briefly, for "blessed are the dead which die in the Lord from henceforth: Yea, saith the Spirit, that they may rest from their labours; and their works do follow them" (Rev. 14:13). Someday, not far from now, new and more glorious chapters in the story of Eric B. Hare will unfold in a far better land where no chapter will have a sad ending. Certainly Eric knew this to be so, for by faith he could grasp the divine promise that "we shall all be changed, in a moment, in the twinkling of an eye, at the last trump: for the trumpet shall sound, and the dead shall be raised incorruptible, and we shall be changed" (1 Cor. 15:51, 52).

To Eric and to his family and to all who knew him, the blessed hope is in looking forward to the sound of the heavenly Trumpeter calling forth from their graves those who have died "in the Lord," and reuniting them with loyal loved ones still living. What a scene! Picture Eric, the trumpeter of the jungle band of Burma, being called forth by the trumpet of God! Imagine the emotions that will be his to gather together the members of his jungle band to play heavenly band music to the glory of God, without even having to rehearse!